Just Beyond the Firelight

ALSO BY ROBERT WALLER

One Good Road Is Enough:
Essays by Robert James Waller

Iowa: Perspectives on Today and Tomorrow
IOWA STATE UNIVERSITY PRESS

The Bridges of Madison County
Slow Waltz in Cedar Bend
WARNER BOOKS, INC.

Just Beyond the Firelight

STORIES AND ESSAYS BY ROBERT JAMES WALLER

Iowa State University Press / Ames

Robert James Waller is professor of business management at the University of Northern Iowa, Cedar Falls.

Most of the material in this book appeared in somewhat different form in the *Des Moines Register* and is reprinted with permission.

♾ Printed on acid-free paper in the United States of America

First edition, 1988
Second printing, 1989
First paperback edition, 1989
Second printing, 1991
Third printing, 1992
Fourth printing, 1993
Fifth printing, 1993
Sixth printing, 1993
Seventh printing, 1993
Eighth printing, 1993
Ninth printing, 1993
Tenth printing, 1993
Eleventh printing, 1993
Twelfth printing, 1993

Library of Congress Cataloging-in-Publication Data

Waller, Robert
    Just beyond the firelight : stories and essays / by Robert Waller.
—1st ed.
        p. cm.
ISBN 0-8138-0163-X — ISBN 0-8138-0167-2 (pbk.)
    1. Waller, Robert—Friends and associates. 2. Waller, Robert. —Journeys. 3. Iowa—Biography. 4. Educators—Iowa—Biography. 5. Musicians—Iowa—Biography. I. Title.
CT275.W2534A3   1988
814'.54—dc19   88–12790
                                                                                              CIP

FOR GEORGIA ANN; RACHAEL; RUTH; ROBERT, SR.; GERALD;

CHARLIE; THE RIVERS; LEONARD; SAMMY; ED; ROADCAT;

THE WIZARD . . . AND IOWA.

Contents

Intricate Dances

Going Soft upon the Land

Worldly Things

Foreword

"IOWANS SHOULD REALIZE THAT ROBERT WALLER IS ONE OF OUR MOST PRODUCTIVE NATURAL RESOURCES," the letter in the *Des Moines Sunday Register* said. It was one of nearly thirty letters in praise of Robert Waller's canoe-trip series, "Going Soft upon the Land and Down along the Rivers," printed for eight consecutive days in the *Register* in August 1987.

Happily, such letters show that Iowans are beginning to recognize Robert Waller as a kind of state treasure, a rare natural resource whose essays deserve serious attention.

Of what is this natural resource composed, then? That's no small or easy question. Robert Waller's talents and interests at first glance don't seem compatible. How many business management consultants played—as starters—on a college basketball team? How many business school deans play and sing their own songs in crowded bars on weekends? How many mathematics scholars write essays about canoe trips down small rivers? How many professors of management are romantics or, maybe more accurately, mystics?

"Multi-faceted" seems too tame, as does the now-trite "Renaissance man." I've come to see Robert Waller's character as a large old house with a room for practically every taste and interest.

Let me offer a tour.

First, the athlete. A bona-fide jock, a first-string high school and college basketball player. He still holds the record for the most career points (1,600) made at Rockford High—from which he graduated in 1957. He was named All–North Central Conference in 1962 for his playing at UNI. Except for the essay "Jump Shots," he doesn't talk about this part of his past much, but others do. He's remembered for his extraordinary jump shot, his scoring ability, his agility on the floor. If he were more jock-like (and maybe at least a couple of inches taller), he could have played for the pros.

Second, the songwriter. He began writing songs in graduate school, and within five years took his songs to Nashville, where they told him he could indeed make a living writing country and western songs. But they also told him that too many of his songs weren't marketable. "We're selling toothpaste down here," they said. "Go back home and be a college professor." He did just that, but continued to write songs.

He's written dozens of memorable lines, lines that still give me shivers. From "Ben Johnson's Daughter," one of his earliest songs: "Still one last single leaf remains/Though battered by the bitter winds/And ragged now from times gone by/It hopes that summer will come again/But somehow knows it never will."

From the same song, there's a great comment on boyhood: "My world was circumscribed by the distance I could walk/And still be home by suppertime."

And this, from "Texas Jack Vermilion": "He might have been a mountain man in the high evergreens/Might have sailed with Captain Cook, out around the Horn/Might have been a drover, on the Goodnight Loving Trail/But the dice were rolled, he's fifty years old/And Mexico fades like a dream."

He writes about some of this in "Ridin' Along in

Safety with Kennedy and Kuralt" and "Where the Wizard Lives." Many of the short poems sprinkled through his essays were originally written as songs, nearly all of which he performed regularly for Iowa audiences. Sometimes these old houses have anterooms, so add singer and musician to songwriter.

And scholar. Waller was Senior Research Fellow at the Battelle Memorial Institute in Columbus, Ohio, in 1975–76. He has published in *Decision Sciences, International Journal of General Systems, Business Horizons,* and monographs from the Battelle Institute. A long article, "Comparing and Combining Structural Models of Complex Systems" (published in *IEEE Transactions on Systems, Man, and Cybernetics*), was selected in 1979 as one of the ten best articles in the world for its contribution to general systems research. The three essays under "Worldly Things" and the economic development portions of "Going Soft upon the Land" are direct descendants of his scholarly writing.

And administrator. For seven years he ran the UNI School of Business as its dean, got it up and pulling a heavy load, like a balky draft horse. UNI's vice president for academic affairs has been quoted as saying, "Our School of Business was at a critical state when Waller took over as dean. He gave it strong impetus. He has a keen sense of quality. His recruiting of staff has been very impressive."

What always amazed me more than his accomplishments as dean was his ability to come home on a Friday night, shed his adminstrator's costume (an impeccable three-piece suit), climb into jeans and boots, haul out his guitar, toss back a few beers, and sing: "She was sweet apple blossoms in her old faded jeans/Forty-five years old and shinin' like the sun/And the touch of her hand on your face was like the breeze/Blowin' sweet and clear, when the long day is done." However bizarre this seemed to his colleagues, to Waller it seemed perfectly natural, even inevitable.

Some Friday nights would find him home by six after a day of meetings with university faculty; by eight he was stomping around a stage in his boots setting up a sound system for a night of singing Lightfoot, Dylan, Simon, Cohen, Waller. . . .

And traveler. He has consulted for the government of Saudi Arabia, for firms in India, and all over America. He vacations regularly in Jamaica, St. Maarten, Switzerland, France. His travels fire his imagination—the more exotic, the better. He implored UNI graduates to travel widely and well in "Romance," his UNI graduation address. And "The Boy from the Burma Hump"—published for the first time here—reveals both his admiration for Charlie Uban and his love of foreign cultures.

He once wrote me a long letter from the Hotel Montien in Bangkok, Thailand, in which he says, "This is 'way out there.' You feel it and sense it and taste it. . . . I am so overwhelmed by the constant sense of wonderment that I am really here, doing this, living the images from my childhood, from my reading . . . I am, well, wrapped in it, covered by it. It is strange but yet so familiar. I have moved like a shadow through such places before."

Like a shadow, and maybe like a wizard. For, most of all, Robert Waller is a mystic. As he says openly in "The Importance of Vision," "if you can't count it, it's probably important." Or as I've heard him say a dozen times, if it can be measured, it's probably not worth measuring.

For Waller has virtually no faith in counting, in the statistical, quantitative view of things. For him, it's magic that matters. He uses other names for it: romance, intuition, the great blue heron and the wizard of "Going Soft upon the Land and Down along the Rivers." It's central to his vision; it informs everything he does.

I won't presume to try to explain it. In fact, it can't be explained except through images and metaphors. It's contained in many of his song lyrics, probably most directly in this stanza from "Some Play the Hornpipes":

> Some play the hornpipes, others play the reels,
> Some may play a waltz, or an old dancing tune
> But I am bound to follow the wizard as he runs,
> In ever-growing circles, tracing rings around the moon.

Where does the wizard run? Where might the great blue heron be found? And where do all these traits come together to form the man, Robert Waller? For all three questions, the answer is the same: just beyond the firelight.

SCOTT CAWELTI

Preface

THIS IS ALL QUITE UNEXPECTED. The book, that is. Frankly, I'm a little amazed and somewhat overwhelmed by the whole affair. Don't get me wrong; I'm not engaging in some disingenuous lurch toward false modesty here. It's just that, well, the book sort of came out of the night, rapped on my chamber door, and took me by surprise.

How it came about is a story worth telling, for it illustrates how chance can prevail where a well-planned strategy undoubtedly would have failed.

When James Gannon, editor of the *Des Moines Register*, was visiting the campus of the University of Northern Iowa in the summer of 1983, he casually mentioned that he wished more Iowans would write for the *Register*. I stored that away under "Interesting Things to Try Sometime," a file I seldom open, and went on my way.

A month or so after hearing Gannon's comment, I was watching Charles Kuralt's Sunday morning television program. Seeing Kuralt took me back to a bar in Bloomington, Indiana, where I had once met him, quite by chance. The meeting had some interesting twists to it, so I went to my desk and began writing. By the next day, I had finished "Ridin' Along in Safety with Kennedy and Kuralt."

Never having written anything like that before, I had no way to judge its worth. But, secure in my position and with myself, I sent it off, wondering. The following Sunday I picked up the *Register*, and there was my story in the editorial section.

I received some nice mail about the piece from readers of the paper, and my friends who know something in a formal way about writing offered what seemed to be genuine encouragement, if not praise. That summer, I gave the university commencement address and spoke on the notion of romance.

Off I went to India to do some work, and by ways more circuitous than you care to know, the address was published in the *Register* while I was gone. That piece drew heavy mail, all of it kind beyond the merits of the essay. After that, I began to send, irregularly, other pieces to Gannon and then to James Flansburg, editor of the *Register*'s editorial section. They have been good enough to publish most of them.

After "Slow Waltz for Georgia Ann" appeared in 1986, Bill Silag, Managing Editor of Iowa State University Press, called and asked if I might be interested in doing my autobiography for them. I joshed with Bill about that effort being a little premature. He then suggested we think about an essay collection that, in a rather loose way, contained some autobiographical threads.

That excited me. As you will see, I have tried to write lovingly about people and things and places and animals I care deeply about. My pleasure at seeing the book published is not so much for myself, but for them. Some are still alive, others were gone years ago, and two died while the book was being written. All the stories are true, all the events transpired. The innocent have not been spared by a change of names.

So you'll get to know Sammy Patterson, old duffer and ace billiards player, who was one of my teachers in a peculiar fashion. And there's Charlie Uban, who hammered C-47 cargo planes through the wind and snow of the southern Himalayas, when the world had lost control. My friend and advisor, The Wizard, appears here and there, along with other dancers and dreamers. You'll meet them all, and they all, I think, are worth meeting.

There is an obvious temptation, when looking over a piece written earlier in your life, to update and change, to bring current skills and standards to bear. I have resisted that temptation. The articles appear in their original forms, except for a place or two where I have corrected an obvious factual error.

All writers are in debt, one way or the other. For the laughter and the wild times, and for advice that was almost too gentle on occasion, my good friend and musical partner for twenty-four years, Scott Cawelti, deserves my applause. Judy Sutcliffe's rapid-fire energy and incredibly creative mind helped me through some serious problems on several of the pieces. Linda Kettner and Shirley Koslowski read early drafts of the long river essay and offered both encouragement and suggestions.

Betty Anderson, my administrative assistant for six years, acted as cheerleader throughout and typed several of the pieces, before I acquired my word processor. John Olson of the Iowa Department of Natural Resources provided me with much information on water quality in Iowa and also copies of handwritten notes from J. Salyer's journal on the Shell Rock River.

Then, of course, there are James Gannon and James Flansburg from the *Register*. They published essays that might be considered too risky for a paper without the stature and the sense of itself that the *Register* has.

And Bill Silag stood his ground and believed in the project from the start, even when doubters seemed to have the upper hand. Finally, I must sincerely and profoundly thank the hundreds of people, from Iowa and elsewhere, who wrote long, wonderful letters to me expressing their enjoyment in reading the pieces when they first appeared. They reassured me that I am not alone in my sometimes oblique view of things, that, after all, romance and rivers are where the real truth lies, and, most important, that these stories are worth the telling.

ROBERT JAMES WALLER

Cedar Falls, Iowa
Winter 1987

Intricate Dances

Slow Waltz for Georgia Ann

I HEAR THE SLAP OF THE CLAY AS YOU WORK IT, LATE IN THE NIGHT. And I know you are there in your studio, in bib overalls, an old sweater, and heavy work shoes. Soon your wheel will begin to turn in time with some faint and distant music, and the teapots and lamps and goblets will lift effortlessly from nothing more than moistened earth.

So the night wind moves the trees outside, and I remember you from a college-town party hall. Twenty-eight years ago now. Through the smoke and across the tables we were taken with each other from the start. An enchanted evening. Our own private cliché. The sort of thing people don't believe in anymore.

And then years later I watch you. Coming toward me on your dancer's walk through the early twilight of high-plateau India. Your sari is silk, and blue above your sandals, your earrings are gold and dangling long. Heads above bodies in white wicker chairs along the veranda of the West End Hotel turn as you pass. Your already dark skin has been made even darker from our days in the Bangalore sun, and there are speculations about you. An Indian man asks, "Is she Moroccan?" "No," I reply. "She is Iowan."

I take another beer from the refrigerator, hoping you stay in your studio a while longer. I want to sit here by myself, listening to the muffled sounds of your hands at work, and think about what it means to be married to you for twenty-five years. In another month, it will have been that long.

I grew up dreaming of rivers and music and ancient cities and dark-haired women who sang old songs in cafés along the Seine. You were raised to be a wife and a beauty, and you probably would have been satisfied, maybe happier, with a more conventional man. At least it took you a long time to discover what I am up to and to know this race I run, a race between death and discovery. You were plainly discomfited by my lurching from one passion to another, from basketball to music, from the academy to think tanks, from city to city, from the solitude of my study to the dark bars where I am at home with my instruments.

Early on, with me dancing along early morning beaches and feeding my demons, it was clear that you would need a life of your own if this marriage were to flourish. That was your hardest struggle. It almost broke us apart. But you found something in the clay, something that quietly said, "This is me."

And I knew we had won when the woman at the cocktail party gushed: "Oh, you must be the potter's husband!" Inside of me, at that moment, I shouted in celebration. Not for myself, or even for us, but for you. Chrysalis had died, you had become. Now the potter's work and the potter's trade keep you centered like the clay.

Love? I cannot analyze that. It is of a piece. Taken apart, it becomes something else, and the gull-like melody that is ours disappears. But even in our difficult times, times when we took suitcases down from closet shelves and stared at each other in anger, love was there.

Liking is another matter. I can get a hold on that. Most of all, I think, I like you for the good-natured understanding you worked so hard to acquire, even if that understanding sometimes borders on wavering tolerance.

You understand the need to live with old furniture and rusted cars and only two kitchen cabinets and rough wooden floors and vacuum cleaners that don't vacuum and clothes washers that operate correctly only when the tab from a beer can is stuck just so behind the dial, so that a little money will be there when I yell over the side of the loft, "Let's go to Paris!"

Remember the time I was in graduate school and we had less than $100 in the bank, when I considered trading our doddering Volkswagen for a guitar? You crinkled your face, looked serious, and said, with no hint of the scold, "How will we get to the grocery store?" You said only that. And I was grateful.

You tolerate one side of the living room stacked with music equipment, while my canoe full of camping gear and two cats tenants the other side, stretching from one corner over to where it inelegantly mingles with an amplifier, several microphone stands, and old suitcases full of cords and other necessary truck. I am working on the gunnels and mumbling about river maps I can't find and rotten weather and wizards I am going out to search for. Over dinner, you smile softly and ask, "How long do you think the canoe will be in the living room?" The point is made. I will move it out tomorrow. Or maybe the day after.

You are older now. I can see that if I look hard. But I don't. I have always seen you in soft focus. I see you standing in the winter on a great stretch of deserted beach in the Netherlands Antilles brushing your long and freshly washed hair in the sea wind from Venezuela. I see you in khaki and sandals at the waterfront café in French Marigot listening to an island band play a decent imitation of vintage American rock 'n' roll. Chuck Berry and ol' Jerry Lee were part of our courting years, and we grin at the aging lyrics—"Long distance information, give me Memphis, Tennessee. . . . "

I glance over and see you beside me at blackjack tables around the world. Was it in Vegas where you wore a long gold dress and the fur coat you bought for $50 at a second-hand clothing shop? I think so. We played all night, I remember that. Guilty though you felt about buying anything made of fur, you were the perfect 1930s vamp as I counted cards in my blue suspenders.

Or I look up ever so slightly from the fingerboard of my jazz guitar and watch as you play the second chorus of "Gone with the Wind," the one where you do the little two-fingered runs I like so well. You are hunched over the keyboard, lightly swaying in pink and white and wearing dark glasses. The sun hammers down, while people dance, by a pool, on the Fourth of July, in Chicago.

And you are sleepy in bed and lit so gently by early light when I bring you coffee on high, hard winter mornings, while the wood stove putters around trying to douse the cold of the night. I have been up for hours reading and writing. You are no morning person, so talk must come later. Still, I hover around, clumsily, just to look at you and smell the warm, perfumed scent of your body.

It seems I have spent a lifetime running toward you. I have tossed in my bed in Arabian desert towns and wanted you. I have stared off midnight balconies in deep Asia, watching dhows older than me tug at their moorings and long for the thrash of coastal waters, missing you and wondering about you.

I am uneasy at being nearly thirty-hours' flying time from you. That's too far. Then, over the miles and across the oceans, through a thousand airports, I am home, wrinkled and worn, and you are there with a single rose and a small sign that says, "Welcome Home, Captain Cook, Welcome Home." Late into the night we laugh as I take the gold and silver presents from my battered suit-case.

I have trusted the years, and I was right to do so. They brought me you. We have watched others' lives intertwine and then unravel. But we have held together. At least for this life, in this time.

Yet I am haunted by the feeling that we might not meet again, that this might be just our one moment in the great sweep of things. Once, as I lay on the floor, breathing through oxygen tubes, looking past the somber faces of paramedics, I saw your tears, and I felt a great sadness, worrying not about myself, but rather that I might not find you again in the swirling crowds out there in the centuries to come. It was the loss of you, not life, that I feared.

For we have come by different ways to this place. I have no feeling that we met before. No déjà vu. I don't think it was you in lavender by the sea as I rode by in A.D. 1206 or beside me in the border wars. Or there in the Gallatins, a hundred years ago, lying with me in the silver-green grass above some mountain town. I can tell by the natural ease with which you wear fine clothes and the way your mouth moves when you speak to waiters in good restaurants. You have come the way of castles and cathedrals, of elegance and empire.

If you were there in the Gallatins, you were married to a wealthy rancher and lived in a grand house. I was a gambler at the table or the mountain man at the bar or the fiddler in the corner, playing a slow waltz to his memories. The dust from your carriage was of more value than my life in those days, and it drowned me in longing and sullied my dreams as you passed by in the street. Somehow, though, for this life and this time, we came together. You taught me about caring and softness and intimacy. The task before me was to teach you about music. And dreams. And how to savor the smell of ancient cities and the sound of cards whispering across green felt. This I have done.

So I rest secure knowing that you have learned and that, in another time, you might recognize me coming across the street of some gambler's town, in high brown boots with an old fiddle case over my shoulder, as your carriage moves by in the dust. And perhaps you will smile and nod and, for a strange and flickering moment, you will remember how the waves of January wash the sea wall at Marigot.

A Rite of Passage in Three Cushions

I'VE ALWAYS LIKED PERSONAL-SIZED HEROES. In the early 1950s, when other boys were fawning over Duke Snider or Rocky Marciano, I was deifying Sammy Patterson in an unpretentious room on the main street of Rockford, Iowa.

I can still see him. Baggy shirt and pants. Flask protruding from his right hip pocket. He walked slowly and spoke quietly. But when he bent over the billiard table, his cue moved with the silent accuracy of an archer's arrow. His stroke was smooth and sure, and the result was never harsh, just the soft click of ivory against ivory, as the balls moved in complex patterns over the green cloth. He must have been about 60 then.

This was no fancy parlor where Sammy practiced his trade. No tuxedos, no leanings toward precious respectability with big prize money and women in evening gowns. Here, in Gerald Braga's "The Sportsman," pool was pool and billiards was billiards.

In case you have led a life more sheltered than I care to imagine, pool tables have pockets, billiard tables do not. At least this was true in the world in which I grew up. Billiards is played with three balls. Two white, one red. One of the white balls has a small spot on it to differentiate it from the other. One player shoots the "clear" and the other commands the "spot." The object is to make your cue ball hit each of the other two balls in one shot. A carom, in other words. Sound easy? It is not. Billiards is a game of physics, geometry, composition, skill, and treachery.

And Sammy was good, very good, at it. He covered three angles on each shot. Make the carom. Set yourself up for the next shot. Leave nothing for your opponent in case you miss. He taught me just about everything he knew, including how to hold ordinary pool players in infinite disdain, as I followed him around the table, night after night, dragging a cue as tall as I was.

I entered Sammy's world through a rite of passage. All cultures have these, and mine was no different. One Sunday morning my parents and I drove over from Rockford to have dinner with my grandparents in Charles City. After we arrived and my mother had hurried off to the kitchen, my dad looked at me with a glint of wickedness in his eyes and said, "Let's go up to the Elks Club."

For an 11-year-old boy, this was tantamount to being invited into manhood. It was the big leagues. Locked doors, a bar, silence on a Sunday morning, rumors of slot machines in the basement, and the smell of booze, smoke, and modest indiscretion left over from the previous night's party. It was a man's world. Women were invited for the parties sometimes; children were invited never, except for the annual Christmas bash, when the place, the language, and the behavior were sanitized.

My dad walked past the bar, flipped on the light over a pool table without breaking stride, and stood before the long racks of cues. Like a scholar gently perusing books in a sacred library, he ran his fingers lightly over the cues, pausing now and then to turn one and look at the number engraved on it indicating its weight.

He selected two, rolled them on the table to make sure they were straight, and casually slipped a few balls, including the cue ball, from the leather pockets. The training began. "Never, ever, shoot hard, except in special cases." "Here, spread the last three fingers of your left hand on the table, crook your first finger over to meet your thumb, and control the cue by running it through the circle made by your finger and thumb. Only amateurs put all five fingers down and run the cue over the place between the finger and the thumb." "Here's how English works." "Here are some tough shots and how to handle them."

It went on like that. For several weeks, each time we drove to Charles City on a Sunday morning, we shot pool. My dad was a fine player. I learned from watching him. Learned the language and the moves. Learned to take it seriously.

After the training, I was turned loose at Braga's place (we never called it "The Sportsman"). Braga and my dad were fishing buddies, so who knows what kind of pact was forged to assure my mother that, indeed, I would be all right there behind the steamed-over windows, lost in the thick smoke, and subject to the wild yelling and pointed oaths that came from the card room in the back, the room that had a sign saying "No Miners" tacked to its swinging-door entrance. (I remember pondering the fact that there was not a mine within 100 miles of Rockford.)

It was a dime a cue, loser pay, and it nearly always was crowded. My pool and fishing crony, Dennis Parker, and I headed for there every afternoon when we escaped from school. And, of course, weekends were best. On Fridays we raced to Braga's, put a nickel in the pinball machine, hoisted it up on our toes when Gerald wasn't looking, and ran up 200 free games, enough to keep us going for hours. One of us shot pool, one played pinball, and then we traded off.

I used to sit in school and dream of the beautiful patterns the pool balls made as they rolled, contemplating strategies for difficult shots. I kept shooting and got better. Pretty soon, I could spend all weekend in Braga's for an outlay of maybe 40 cents, not counting the mustard-smeared hot dogs I ate from the machine that went round and round by the cash register. Sometimes Gerald hired me to rack balls on Saturday nights. I picked up a dollar for the evening doing that and actually showed a profit for my day.

I acquired my own cue for $5 from Kenny Govro. Kenny, it was said, had a bad heart and counted on his American Indian wife, Snow, to support him. He claimed he was giving up pool and billiards, in a fit of anger over losing one night, and sold me the cue.

It was a thing of beauty. Seventeen ounces of light-colored gleaming wood, cork grip, trimmed in ivory. An arrow for the wars that consumed me. It rested quietly in a special, locked rack fastened to a wall inside the card room, until I gently removed it each day and began to shoot pool ("miners" were allowed in the card room to get their private cues).

My mother was worried. Remember, this was only eighteen miles southeast of River City. She could spell trouble, she knew it started with "t," and she knew what that fateful letter rhymed with. But she was overmatched. I shot pool out front, my dad was in the card room playing pinochle, and at least she knew where I was.

The only real concession she demanded, and she stood absolutely firm on this, was that I undress on the back porch and leave my "awful, smelly clothes out there." Those were her words. I thought I smelled just fine, anointed as I was with smoke, mustard stains, cue chalk, and the unmistakable musk of burgeoning skill.

At some point, I don't remember when, I was allowed to try the billiard table. This was another step in the rite of passage, as significant as learning to play pool. The billiard table was Gerald's glory. He kept its smooth, un-marked surface and lively cushions covered with light canvas when it was not in use. The balls were stored safely out of reach in a box behind the front counter. You had to have Gerald's permission to play on the billiard table. Perhaps twenty people held that permission at any time.

There is a beauty about billiards that's hard to explain if you never have played. It's like watching a ballet, or listening to Bach. It contains within it pure form, an aesthetic of motion, point and counterpoint, fugue-like movement, and the sense of a small universe into which one can plunge forever.

It was a different place from the cacophony of the pool tables only a few feet away. A place of silence, of concentration, of men who knew what they were doing. And Sammy Patterson ruled that world with a fearsome and undisputed grip.

The showdown was, I suppose, inevitable. The teacher, the student, the game. There are vectors at work out there that we do not understand, that bring us together in particular settings at chosen times, with the outcomes known only to those curious gods of chance and logic.

If there was a definable cause, though, it had to do with Kenny Govro. Kenny was regarded as the second-best billiards player in town, some distance behind Sammy. Shortly after his announced retirement from the game, he decided to renege on his promise and was casting around one night for someone to play. All he could find was the kid who had bought his cue. Oh well, a little practice to get the rust off. I slaughtered him. Sammy's teaching and the constant practice were working.

Kenny blamed it on the loss of his cue, re-entered retirement, and left Braga's cursing about cues and smart-aleck kids and life in general. My shellacking of Kenny

13

may have convinced Sammy that it was about time to see what the kid could do.

It all came down on one of those hot, humid Iowa evenings in June, around 1953. I was in the general vicinity of 14 by this time. Sammy and I never had really played a serious game. Instead, he would set up shots, show me how to attack them ("medium left English, off the left side of the red ball, hit the side cushion, then the end cushion, then the other side, and it'll head right for that old spot ball down in the corner"), and generally was trying to make a first-class billiards player out of the kid who followed him around.

I can't remember how the game got organized. There always was a certain mating dance that occurred when two good players were going to have at it. But, somehow, the little buttons on the wires overhead where the points were kept got shoved back, and the cues were chalked.

Word had flashed around in that mysterious small-town way that Sammy and I were going to play. Ordinarily, this would not have meant much, but the same communication system had already disseminated the news about my easy victory over Kenny, and a fair amount of interest was generated.

In fact, quite a lot of interest was generated. By the time Sammy and I squared off, some twenty or thirty spectators had gathered. For a 14-year-old boy up against the Master, it was the Coliseum at noon, the sun and the sand, a matter of virility and honor lined out in some distant chant about young men and old lions.

We began. The match was to 500 points. I was on top of my game, running off strings of 20 or more points as my turn came. Sammy was not playing well. Perhaps it was the heat, perhaps it was because he had been conversing intently and at length with his flask while we warmed up. After a while, though, the magic welled up within him, and he began to make some long runs. It worried me. He was capable, I knew, of running off 75 points in one turn. I faltered, lost my confidence for a bit, recovered, and got back into it.

To this day, I can feel what it felt like then—the heat, the sweat, the smoke, the quiet murmuring of the men gathered around, and the old words of my father and Sammy flowing with clarity through my mind ("shoot easy," "high right English," "four cushions and get the red ball back up in the left corner," "if you are going to miss, don't leave him anything").

I began to see that I actually could win. I smelled and tasted the possibility. Teetering there on the brink of manhood, I got down hard and tight and mean. One or two long runs, and I had it. It was over. I couldn't believe it. Sammy looked tired, but I cared only that I had won.

I remember sprinting for home, bursting in and yelling, "I beat Sammy, I beat Sammy." My dad seemed surprised, went downtown to check out the facts, came home and didn't say much, except to congratulate me in a quiet way.

I didn't play much after that. Somehow, it wasn't the same. Mostly, I just strutted around with "Champ" written in invisible letters on my chest. I talked incessantly at home about the victory, and my father kept agreeing that, yes, it was quite a triumph.

A few weeks later, I strolled into Braga's. Dad was lounging against the counter talking with Gerald on a quiet Tuesday night. He grinned at me, "Son, want to play a little billiards?" Now, my dad was not a billiards player, just pool. Oh, he knew the rules and so forth, but he never played much. Cocky, I grinned back, "Sure."

Only Braga was there to see it. We chalked up, cleared the wires, and started. It was no contest.

My dad was a peculiar guy, good at anything requiring hand-eye coordination. He had worked something out with Gerald about practice time and had been bending over that green cloth for scores of hours, unbeknown to me. There was no letting up this time, as he sometimes did when he was beating me at pool in my learning days. He really went after it.

I was both rusty and rattled. He just kept grinning. Gerald watched, jingling coins in his change apron. I got mad and played worse. Dad played better. He scalded me. I refused his offer of a ride home and came sulking in a few hours later.

Other things took over my life. Basketball, falling in love, working. I never played much, if any, pool or billiards again. I came home from college once, went in to visit Gerald, walked around, and saw my old cue out in the public racks. It was battered from being slammed down on the pool tables when the "slop" players missed easy shots. I looked at it. It looked back dolefully, a mistress cast away for prettier things. Like the lovers that we were in an earlier time, we gazed softly at one another for a moment, sharing the memories rich and warm before I turned and walked away.

The lessons come slowly. Sammy died twenty years or so after that night of thunder and victory in Braga's place. Then Gerald went. Then my dad. The four of us were involved in a complicated dance, unchoreographed and intricate, unrehearsed and precise.

They taught me rhythms I have only recently begun to sense, melodies that escaped me until now—that Zen and precision are not at odds, that small universes exist if you acquire the discipline and skill to enter them, and that grace, passion, and an elegance of spirit are all that really matter, whether you're shooting billiards, making love, playing the guitar, winning, or losing.

You see, Gerald Braga didn't run a pool hall in a small

Iowa town. He was the keeper of an academy. Sammy Patterson and my dad were among the faculty, and I, God love them all, had the good fortune to study there in the times when I was small, and tender, and wondering what it was like to be a man.

A Canticle for Roadcat

I HAD A FRIEND . . . AND HIS NAME WAS ROAD-CAT. He was young when I was young and old when I was middle-aged. Still, our lives overlapped for a while, and I am grateful for that.

He was more than a friend, really. Friend and colleague is perhaps a better image. In fact, I sometimes introduced him to strangers as my research associate. We worked together on cold, gray afternoons, poring over books and papers, while the wood stove quietly crackled its way through another Iowa winter.

Sometimes he lay upon my lap and served as a round and honest book rest. He purred and occasionally reached out to turn pages for me, randomly and with a keen appreciation of the virtues surrounding leisurely scholarship. In the spring, as the days warmed, he moved to the desk, clearing a place for himself by pushing to the floor paper, pens, staplers, and other implements of a writer's trade.

He came from a field of long grass behind our house in Columbus, Ohio. Just a few inches in length, he walked along the cement of one of those smarmy subdivisions that make your teeth curl.

A neighbor's child abused him. He fought back, as any of us would, and the child's mother screamed something about rabid cats. My wife observed that the child deserved something more than he got and brought the kitty home for the customary saucer of milk.

I set him on my lap and said, "This is going to be a fine-looking cat." But we were on the move in those times and had already promised our daughter one of the kittens from a litter down the street. So the migrant was fed and sent along.

I sat down to read the paper, glanced up, and he had reappeared on the opposite side of the house at the patio screen door. He looked in at me, and I looked back. He coughed continuously and badly, tried to cry, but the effort was soundless. I picked him up, looked him over with a modest expertise gained from years of living around animals, and said I was taking him to the veterinarian's office.

The examination was lengthy. He had worms, ear mites, fleas, and a serious case of bronchitis. I asked the vet, "Is this a road cat?" The doctor smiled, "This is your genuine road cat."

We drove home together, he and I and, of course, four kinds of medicine in a brown paper bag. He sat on the car seat, small and uncomplaining, watching me, bright face hopeful. The nursery opened. Roadcat had come to stay.

And it is here, before going on, that I must deal with the issue of sentimentality. If I do not come to grips with that, you might dismiss the rest of what I have to say as mawkish and lacking sound perspective.

Humans have an arrogant manner of ranking life, as if some squat, three-level hierarchy of existence were fact instead of intellectual artifice. God by various names is way up there, of course, in the first position. A little further down, just a little, lies humankind. Below that, and far below, according to common belief, rests a great squishy level of everything else. Here, we find plants and animals. Maybe even rivers and mountains.

All right, let's admit that some transcending presence

roams above us. Some call it God, some call it science. Others of us see it as a design so perfect, a great swirling form of truth and beauty and justice and balance, that cosmic ecology might be our term.

That leaves us and the rest. And if you're going to attempt rankings, you better have some criteria, some standards of measurement, to use in making your judgments. The problem is that we humans generate the criteria by which the rankings are made. That's letting the fox in with the chickens, or the cat in with the canary, or us in with beauty. Take your choice.

I read the philosophers sometimes. They have criteria, such as consciousness and the ability to use technology, for determining who and what get to belong to various communities. But I do not trust their judgments, for the reason just mentioned. I prefer to think of civilizations that are, well, just different—separate, but parallel and equal.

And I don't spend much time trying to create workable taxonomies either. Others do that sorting rather competently. But taxonomies always end up looking like hierarchies, and things eventually get a little too classified for my taste.

So I just coast along with the notion of parallel civilizations. It works pretty well for me. Bears and butterflies, trees and rivers. I try to live alongside rather than above them. Our world is fashioned to make this difficult, but I try.

Those of you who see things differently, as a matter of "better than" or "on a higher plane than," are to be pitied. I'm sorry to be so blunt, but I know your view is only one way, and that is down. As such, you miss the grand vistas, the shuddering sense of wonderment that comes from looking out across all the civilizations riding along together on Eddington's great arrow of time.

And so it was with my friend Roadcat. Riding along on the arrow, we turned the days and marked the pages together. We grinned at each other over sunny afternoons on the deck, and, while he rested in the crook of my folded arm, we tilted our furry heads and stared high and hard at the lights of space just before dawn. Green eyes looking. Blue eyes looking. Wondering about ourselves and the others out there looking back.

We did that for twelve years plus a month or so. And we came to care, and care deeply, one for the other. He clearly saw, as I eventually did, that power and exploitation were not part of the reflections from each other's eyes. We came to a position of trust, and, in his wisdom and elegance, that was all he asked.

I violated that trust only once. I must take time to tell you about it, for the event contains the thread of a hard lesson.

Roadcat represented all the classic definitions of beauty and good taste. The long, soft pelage on his back and sides was predominantly black and gray. His chin was an off-white that flowed into creamy tan along his chest and belly. Symmetrically perfect were his markings, and he watched his world through green eyes of great immensity and color. His face was expressive, his conformation perfect.

Given that, it becomes understandable why we fell into the snare of seeing him as an object. When the local cat fanciers association announced a show limited to animals of something called pet quality, we could not resist.

So Roadcat was put into a wire cage and carried off to the show held as part of the Cattle Congress festivities in Waterloo. Along with the sheep and horses and cattle and hogs, the pet-quality cats would have their day in the ring. He was terrified and panting as I carried him through the crowds, past the ferris wheel and midway barkers, past Willie Nelson's touring bus.

Roadcat's world was the forest, the warm place under the wood stove, and a canvas deck chair in the summer. He was content with himself and required no conspicuous recognition to prove his worth. His colleague apparently did require it. My wife, my daughter, and I wore blue t-shirts we had made up for the occasion that said "Road-cat" in bold, black letters across the front.

I watched him closely in the great hall where the judging was held. He was restless in the cage. Finally, he simply lay down and stared directly at me, straight in the eyes. I could see he was disappointed with me, and I was ashamed at having so ruthlessly shattered our mutual respect. Since a time when I was quite young, I have been angered by those public adulations of the human form called beauty contests, and here I was subjecting my friend to exactly that.

Roadcat refused to be an object. Normally temperate and reserved around strangers, he tore at the paper lining his cage on the judging platform, attempted to push his way through the metal top of his containment, and, when the judge put him on a table for all to see, he simply slid onto his back and tried to scratch the well-meaning woman who was to measure his worth.

Suddenly, confusion erupted among the various judges and assistants. A huddle formed around Roadcat, and I went forward to see what was happening. One of the assistant judges had lodged a complaint, contending that Roadcat was a purebred and did not belong in a pet-quality show. The supreme arbiter was consulted, and her verdict was this: Roadcat was the prototype image of a breed called Maine coon cats, descendents of random matings between domestic cats who rode the sailing ships from Europe and wild cats of the New World.

In the American cat shows of the late nineteenth century, the Maine coon cats were the most treasured breed of all. The head judge explained that if this had been 1900, Roadcat would have been the perfect specimen.

But humans are never satisfied with nature, and the Maine coon cats, for reasons not clear to either Roadcat or me, had been bred over the decades to have longer noses. Thus Roadcat was held to be something of a relic, slightly out of date, and was allowed in the show.

He scored high on appearance. The judge said, "He has a wonderful coat, a beautiful face, and the largest, prettiest green eyes I have ever seen." But, sliding and fighting and slashing out for the nearest human jugular vein within reach, he received a failing grade on the personality dimension and was awarded a fourth-place ribbon. Those green eyes brimmed with nasty satisfaction when the judge said, "I'll bet he's not like this at home, is he?"

Back through the midway, past the ferris wheel, past Willie Nelson's bus, and home to the woods. He was disinterested in his remarkable heritage, slept away his terror, and had nothing to do with any of us for some time. Gradually, he accepted my apologies, and our friendship warmed. But he made me work on re-crafting our trust as though it were a fine piece of furniture.

Roadcat was good-natured about most things, though, and seemed to enjoy the little inanities we created around his presence. On pasta nights, his name was changed temporarily to Roadicotta. When my wife, Georgia, held her seasonal pottery sales at our home, he charmed the customers by finding a large pot in which to sit and look out at the commotion. He became "The Retailer" on those occasions. He was "The Chief Inspector" for anything new that came into the house or onto the property, including musical instruments, canoes, and furnaces. In his later years, we called him "The Old Duffer" or "The Big Guy." But mostly he went by Roadie.

He even tolerated the nonsense of my singing songs appropriate to the can of food he and I chose each morning. Seafood Supper? I sang a verse of an old whaling song to the pitch of the electric can opener. How about Country Style for Cats? That got him "San Antonio Rose" in B-flat major, and Elegant Entré was served with a sprinkling of Cole Porter.

The undergrowth and woodland trails around our house were Roadcat's beat. He was a hunter, but not a killer. Now and then smaller creatures died from fright or the initial pounce when he caught them, yet I never saw him intentionally kill anything. Not even the night crawlers he brought to me after heavy rains. He plopped them down on a small throw rug, flipped it over to hamper their escape, and seemed pleased with himself.

The chipmunk was very much alive in the summer of 1986 when Roadie strolled through the front door and dropped it. The little guy hit the carpet running, dashed through a pile of old magazines, and disappeared in the general vicinity of the fireplace.

Judging that the chipper would not eat much, I was content to let him stay. The rest of the family, as usual, thought I was deranged. So, after four days of moving furniture, we flushed the poor fellow. The male dog nailed him to the floor in one of those wild scenes that seem to occur only at our house in the woods. Roadcat watched the entire battle with detached interest. Revenge for the cat-show humiliation finally was his.

In his habits he was careful, in his ways he was gentle. He found our dogs inelegant to the point of being despicable, but he liked the little female kitty that came along some years after he joined the craziness that is ours. He smiled tolerantly when she tried to nurse him and, through the years, gently washed her with a pink and tireless tongue.

Roadcat asked for little other than consideration and respect. He ate what was offered and left our food alone, except for my lunchtime glass of milk resting unattended on the table. He could not resist that. Turning around, I would find him sitting by the glass, licking a milk-covered paw.

That was his only sin, and I reached a compromise with him on the matter by providing him occasionally with a little milk in an old jelly glass decorated with etchings of Fred Flintstone. I think Fred reminded him of earlier times, before humans developed the technology of killing to a high and ludicrous art, when his saber-toothed cousins left no doubt about the equality of things. When he thought of that delicious state of affairs, it made the milk taste even better, and he lingered over it, humming to himself about woodlands and cliffs and open meadows turning yellow in the light of a younger sun.

The early bronchitis had taken most of his voice. So when he wanted attention, he would lie on my computer printer while I typed, purr loudly, and look directly into my face. If that failed, he escalated his tactics by jumping into the box holding the printer paper and tearing it off the machine. Finally, if I was so insensitive as to further ignore his requirements, he would race around the house, across my desk, along the balcony railing, and, eventually, onto my lap. He seldom failed in these efforts.

I watched him turn a little more gray here and there, but I suppressed melancholy thoughts of the inevitable. Roadcat maintained a youngness of spirit and, even in his latter days, could race thirty feet up a tree on any crisp spring morning when he felt like doing so. Yet, as we read Barbara Tuchman's *Stillwell and the American Experience in China* together in the last months of his life, I could almost sense something as he purred his way through the pages. I would lift my eyes from the book, smile at him, and softly stroke his head, which he always acknowledged by a slight increase in the intensity of his purring.

In late September of 1987, I caught a slight hesitation in his leap to the basement table where I placed his food, safe from the growling hunger of the dogs. If I had not shared that breakfast time with him all those hundreds of mornings, I would not have noticed anything. But it was there—a slight, ever-so-slight, hesitation, as if he had to gather himself physically for what should have been an easy leap.

Simultaneously, he seemed to be eating a little less than was normal for him. The usual pattern was that he would eat about one-third of the can of food on the first serving. Then the female cat, who deferred to his seniority, took her turn. Later, Roadcat would come by and finish whatever was left.

But the rhythm faltered. There always was something in the dish at the end of the day. And sometimes he ate nothing after I ladled out the food. His face was thinning a bit, and his coat lost a little of its sheen.

I was about to make an appointment at the veterinarian's when one morning he did not appear for his dawn excursion. It was his custom to come lie near my pillow at first light and wait for me to rise and let him out. The routine was invariant, and the morning it was broken I felt an unpleasant twinge in my stomach.

I searched the house and found him lying in a chair in the back bedroom upstairs. I knelt down beside him, spoke softly, and ran my hand over his fur. He purred quietly, but something was not right.

While waiting for the vet's office to open, I remembered the previous evening. He had seemed strangely restless. He would get on my lap, then down again, then return for another cycle of the same thing. He did that five times, and I remarked to my wife that it was something of a record. The last time he walked up my chest and rubbed his cheek against mine. Though he was always pleasantly affectionate, such a gesture was a little out of the ordinary. He was trying to tell me that something was amiss, that it was almost over.

The initial diagnosis was a kidney problem, which is not unusual in older animals. After a few days, we brought him home. He was terribly weak and could scarcely walk. I laid him on a wool poncho, where he stayed the entire night.

In the morning, I carried him to his litter box in the basement and set him down by it. He seemed disoriented and stumbled. I noticed his right leg was limp and curled underneath him when he sat.

Back to the doctor. An X-ray disclosed a large tumor around his heart, which had resulted in a stroke the previous night that paralyzed his right side and left him blind. Wayne Endres is a kind and patient man, but I could see he was working at the edge of his technology.

The following day, a Wednesday, Wayne called with his report. If it had only been a stroke, we might have worked our way out of it, even though cats don't recover from such things easily. But clearly, the tumor was large and growing, and there was little to be done. It was up to me, of course. But Wayne's quiet voice carried the overtones of despair when he said, "Roadcat is not doing well." He refused to offer hope. There wasn't any, and Wayne Endres is an honest man.

Here, at this point, the thunder starts, and civilizations that are normally parallel begin to intersect and become confused. Roadie and I shared a common language of trust, respect, and love, made visible by touching and aural by our private mutterings to one another. But, as it should be, the language of caring is a language of imprecision and is not designed for hard and profound choices.

I had no set of alternatives rich enough to evade the issue and none available that could even ameliorate it. And how could I understand what decision rules lay beating softly in the imprints of Roadcat's genetic spirals? For all I knew, they might be superior to mine, probably were, but I could not tell.

I know how I want to be treated under those dire conditions. But what right did I have to assume that so ancient a civilization as Roadcat's bears the same values as mine? How could I presume to judge when the standards are someone else's and I had not been told?

Surely, though, notions of dignity and suffering must be common to all that lives, whether it be rivers or butterflies or those who laugh and hold your hand and lie with you in autumn grass. So, gathering myself as best I could, I drove slowly through a red and yellow sunset toward Wayne Endres's clinic.

Someone once defined sentimentality as too much feeling for too small an event. But events are seldom small when you're dealing with civilizations. And they are never small when you're dealing with true companions.

My friend and colleague from all the years and gentle moments lay on a table with white cloth-like paper under him. I sat down, and at the sound and smell of me, he raised his head, straight up came his ears, and his nose wrinkled. Though the room was brightly lit, his brain kept sending a false message of darkness, and the pupils of his green eyes dilated to the maximum as he strained for the light.

He had lost half his body weight. I touched him along the neck, and there was a slight sound. He was trying to purr, but fluid in his throat would not allow it. Still, he wriggled his nose and tried to send all the old signals he knew I would recognize.

I nodded to Wayne and put my face next to that of my friend, trying somehow to convey the anguish I suffered for him and for myself, for my ignorance of right and wrong, and for my inability to know what he might want in these circumstances. I spoke softly to him, struggling with desperate intensity to reach far and across the boundaries of another nation, seeking either affirmation or forgiveness. When all that is linear failed me, I called down the old language of the forest and the plains to tell him, once and finally, of my gratitude for his simply having been.

And I wondered, as did S. H. Hay, "How could this small body hold/So immense a thing as death?"

Eventually, his head lowered, and it was done. Georgia and I carried him home in a blanket and buried him in the woods along one of the trails where he earned his living.

For some days after, I swore I would never go through that again. If it came to euthanasia, I would refuse to be present. I have changed my mind. You owe that much to good companions who have asked for little and who have traveled far and faithfully by your side.

Roadcat didn't just live with us. He was a spirited participant in the affairs of our place. He was kind to us, and we to him. I remember, when I came home in the evenings, how he would move down the woodland path toward me, grinning, riding along on his little stiff-legged trot, tail held high with a slight curl at the tip. I'd hunker down, and we would talk for a moment while he rolled over on his back and looked at me, blinking.

Georgia and I put the shovel away, walked back into

the darkness, and stood by the little grave. By way of a farewell, she said, "He was a good guy." Unable to speak, I nodded and thought she had said it perfectly. He was, indeed, a good guy. And a true friend and colleague who rode the great arrow with me for a time, helping me turn the pages in some old book while the wood stove quietly crackled its way through the winter afternoons of Iowa.

Jump Shots

IN A DAKOTA FEBRUARY, THE WIND NEVER RESTS. Neither do the basketball fans. Both are howling as I bring the ball upcourt in the North Dakota State University fieldhouse. Old patterns before me. Stewart shouting instructions from the sideline. Holbrook loping ahead and to the right. Spoden, our all-American center, struggling for position in the lane. Head fake left, and the man guarding me leans too far. Dribble right. Double screen by Holbrook and McCool. Sweat and noise, smell of popcorn. See it in slow motion now. Behind the screen into the air, ball over my head, left hand cradling it, right hand pushing it, slow backward spin as it launches. Gentle arc.
. . .

The ball just clears the telephone wire and bounces off the rim of the basket as I land on hard-packed dirt in the silence of an Iowa summer evening. Miles from the wind, years before the Dakotas. Bored with school and small-town life at 13, I have decided to become a basketball player. Absurd. Five feet 2 inches tall, 110 pounds.

I am untroubled by the impossibility of it all. Day after day, night after night in the weak glow of the back porch light, the ball goes up. One hundred more shots, and I'll quit. Maybe 200. Can't stop until I have five straight from twenty feet.

Freshman year. I try out for the high-school team,

which is just not done by freshmen. Freshmen are supposed to play on the junior-high team. That's understood. I take a pounding, mentally and physically, from the upperclassmen. Yet, into the evenings, wearing gloves in late autumn, I work jump shots around the telephone wire. Merlin, the school janitor, ignores the rules and lets me in the gym at 7 a.m. on Saturdays. I shoot baskets all day, with a short break for lunch.

The Big Day. Twelve will be selected to suit up for the games. I feel that I have a chance. I have hustled and listened and learned. But about twenty people are trying to make the team, a lot of them are seniors, and there is the whole question of whether a freshman even ought to be out there. At the end of practice, the coach has us informally shoot baskets while he walks the gym with a list. Studying it, he begins to call out names, slowly, one every minute or so: "Mehmen" . . . "Clark" . . . "Lossee" . . .

Eleven names have been called; eleven have gone to the locker room to select their uniforms. I can hardly make my shot go up, or dribble, or even think. The coach paces the gym, looks at his list. Three, four minutes go by. He turns: "Waller."

There is silence; I remember it. A freshman? Wait a minute! I trot to the locker room with a feeling that comes only a few times in a life. The locker room is silent, too. I am not welcome, for all those complex reasons having to do with tradition and adolescence and the 1950s' definition of masculinity. Even Clark, the thoughtful one, shakes his head.

The remaining uniform is the largest of the entire lot. The pants can be cinched in to stay up, but the shirt is so big that the arm holes extend down into the pants when it is tucked in. If it weren't so funny, it would be grotesque. But nobody is laughing.

Running through the darkness of a 1953 November evening, squeezing the neatly folded purple and white jersey, I explode through the back porch and into the kitchen. My parents are stunned. They have humored me through all of this, knowing how sensitive I am about my size. But they never expected success.

My dad is concerned for my safety. "Those big guys will make mincemeat out of you." My mother is worried about my schoolwork. But I care only about getting that damn suit to fit. Mother takes enormous tucks in the shoulder straps until the arm holes assume somewhat normal proportions. The armor fits. The warrior is ready.

Our yellow bus rolls through a midwestern winter with Hank at the wheel. St. Ansgar, Greene, Nora Springs, Riceville, Manly, and on and on, through the Corn Bowl Conference. I ride alone in my jeans, green checkered shirt, and engineer boots, ostracized. A good friend of the seniors has been left home because of me. On the bench, I watch closely. The season is not going well.

Gradually, and mostly out of desperation, the coach looks down the bench and says, "Waller, get up here." Occasionally there is a chance for the long jump shot that arcs into the bright lights of a dozen high-school gyms, slicing the net on its way through the basket. The other players are a little kinder to me. By the final game of the season, I am there. I start. We pound up and down the floor at Nashua, winning. I score 12 points. Merlin lets me in the gym the next morning at seven, grinning, with news of the game from the cafe. "Twelve points, huh?"

More time on the dirt in the summer. "Ya, I'll be in for supper in a minute." Can't quit until I hit ten in a row from twenty feet.

Sophomore year. It's a winning season. I start every game. We upset Rudd, a powerhouse, in the county tournament, and the world is colored good. Merlin shows up smiling when I rattle the gym doors on Saturday mornings.

The back-porch light burns late in warm weather. Can't quit until I hit fifteen in a row from twenty feet. My dad has taken an interest in the whole affair by this time and has the telephone wire moved out of the way. Mother worries about my schoolwork and cooks as if I am a one-man harvest gang. I am 5 feet 10 without warning.

Junior year, new coach. Paul Filter has a low tolerance for dolts. He smiles a lot, but his starched white shirts and neatly pressed suits give him away. This is a serious guy. Serious about teaching history, serious about getting young boys in short pants ready for basketball and for life beyond, a life I cannot conceive of.

We have lost most of our starters and struggle through a break-even year, improving as we go, while Filter lovingly calls us "clowns." But the jump shot is there, game after game, in the hot gyms. On some nights twenty of them go in from far outside.

Paul Filter begins to see what I am up to and designs a training program for me in the off-season. Roadwork and push-ups (no high school weight-training programs around in those days). I do 140 push-ups at one time and grow to 6 feet. It's getting serious.

Something, though, is at work that I do not completely understand. This is more than a game. I think deeply about the art and physics of the jump shot and ponder these while I practice. The search for perfection, the ballet-like movement, soft release, gentle arc, the reward.

My last year rolls up, and I ride the momentum of years of steady practice. The jump shot floats through the Iowa winter nights. The points mount up game by game— 39, 38, 45, 34. I play with two people guarding me in most games, three one time. But the roadwork, the push-ups, and, of course, the jump shot are there with enormous force. The other teams are not prepared for someone training at a near-professional level. Mo Parcher and Bill Mitchell grab rebounds, Tommy Ervin sets screens for me, and we win our first 23 games.

Filter keeps teaching. He has long conversations with me about getting athletics into perspective. He is aware that I will have offers to play college basketball, and he is trying hard to get me ready for something more. I sulk when he takes me out of the St. Ansgar game at the end of the third quarter. I have 39 points and have just hit nine out of ten shots in that quarter as we bury the Saints. I want to stay in and break my own single-game scoring record. Filter moves me far down the bench and refuses to even look at me as he coaches nervous and eager sophomores. The next morning he talks long and hard to me about sportsmanship, perspective, and life.

It ends against Greene in the tournaments. We have beaten them twice before, but they dig in and go at us. My long jumper goes in and out with no time left. Over.

A few days later, a letter comes from Bucky O'Connor, coach at the University of Iowa. Can I come to the campus for a visit and see the Fabulous Five play?

My dad and I spend the day with Bucky, go to a game, and exist in the realms of the privileged. Bucky will recruit four players this year, and he wants me to be one of them. My dad soars. He has spent a lifetime of evenings listening to the Iowa ball games.

We sit at the kitchen table and fill in the scholarship forms. Dad and I laugh and talk about jump shots in the Iowa fieldhouse. Mother says only one thing: "I think this boy should go to college to study something, not to play basketball." What? We verbally abuse her, and she stops talking nonsense.

My first jump shot at Iowa is a memorable one.

Early-season scrimmage, and I confidently move down-court. All the old rhythms are in place. I stop, go into the air, perfect timing, great release, and the tallest person I have ever seen knocks the ball back over my head to the other end of the court. Some adjustments will be necessary.

I don't know much about playing defense or even team basketball. The kids from the cement playgrounds of Chicago and Louisville do. "Okay, Waller, you don't get to play on offense anymore until we say so. Whenever the ball changes hands, you go over to the defensive side."

The jump shot is silenced for a while. Nonetheless, the coach says I am the greatest natural shooter he has ever seen. I grin at the word "natural" as I think of those seven o'clock mornings in the gym. Somewhere, Merlin the janitor also grins.

There is, however, something more going on in my 18-year-old head. The feelings are not clear, but they have to do with the words of Paul Filter and my mother. I like Tom Ryan, my humanities teacher, and also a strange little man who teaches literature. I do poorly in school, though, and blame it on basketball. My freshman year drifts by. Everybody exclaims about the jump shot while waiting for me to develop other areas of the game. And Bucky O'Connor is killed in an auto accident.

A ruptured appendix in the summer, a broken finger, and a nasty knee injury early in the fall get me off to a slow start the next year. I am now haunted by these other feelings. I am close to falling in love with a young woman whom I will marry eventually. And the old curiosities from my boyhood, when I read most of the books in the Rockford library, are surfacing.

Other things bother me, too. Somehow a boy's game has been turned into something else. Grown-ups outside the university actually care about our sprained ankles and the quality of our man-to-man defense. I cannot attach the level of importance to winning that seems to be required. Practice and films and practice and films. Locker-room talk in which women fare poorly leaves me cold. The special study sessions for athletes where amazingly accurate information about upcoming examinations is handed out are repugnant. On principle, I refuse to attend these sessions and am laughed at for it. There is something wrong, deadly wrong, and I know it.

I drop out of school. My father is disappointed and hurt in ways he cannot even express. A few months of menial work, and Iowa State Teachers College takes me in. No scholarship, no financial aid. My parents send money, and I work at a local bank. Good basketball in a lower key.

Norm Stewart comes to coach. He teaches me more about defense in three weeks than I have learned in a lifetime. Mostly, aside from keeping your rear end down and staying on the balls of your feet, he teaches me that defense is pride and gives me tough assignments in the games. I like that. It fits the way I am starting to think about the world.

The purple and gold bus rolls through the Midwestern winters with Jack at the wheel. I stand up front in the door well and gather images for the songs and essays to come. The jump shot is still there. But things are different now. I am studying literature, playing the guitar, spending Saturday mornings reading Clarence Darrow's great closing arguments to his juries, and wallowing in all the things that college and life have to offer.

I am so deeply in love with a woman and with music that basketball becomes something I do because people expect me to do it. Seldom do I reach the levels I know I can touch with the jump shot. Oh, there are nights, in Brookings, South Dakota, and Lincoln, Nebraska, when twenty-five feet looks like a lay-up, the way it used to look in Riceville and Manly, and the baskets are there for the taking. Mostly, though, the old magic is gone.

Still, my dad drives down from Rockford on below-zero nights to watch what is left of it. He sits along the west sideline in the old teachers college gym, and, moving downcourt, I can pick his voice out of 4,000 others, "Go get 'em, Bobby." He was there with the same words, years ago, on winter nights in all the Corn Bowl Conference towns.

He calls on a March morning to say that I have made the All–North Central Conference first team. He heard it on the radio, he is pleased, and I am pleased for him. I ignore my remaining eligibility, take some extra courses, and graduate.

There is one final moment, though. The University of Iowa seniors barnstorm after their season is over. Another player and I team up with a group of high school coaches and play them at the Manchester, Iowa, gym for a benefit. It's a good game. We are in it until the last few minutes when our big center fouls out, and I am forced to guard Don Nelson, later of the Boston Celtics. And, for one more night, the jump shot is there, just as it once was. Twelve of them go down from deep on the outside.

The jump shot, with some 2,500 points scribbled on it, has lain unused for over twenty years. It rests in a closet somewhere, with my old schoolbooks and Flexible Flyer sled. I got it out once to show my daughter, who asked about it. It took a few minutes to shine it up, and she watched it flash for a little while in the late-afternoon light of a neighbor's back yard. I put it away again. It was a boy's tool for a boy's game, for growing up and showing your stuff. Merlin knew that.

More than anything, though, and I understand it

clearly now, the jump shot was a matter of aesthetics, an art form for a small-town kid—the ballet-like movement, the easy release, the gentle arc over a telephone wire through the summer nights of Iowa, while my mother and father peered out the back-porch screen door and looked at each other softly.

Excavating Rachael's Room

LIKE SOME RUMPLED ALIEN ARMY AWAITING MARCHING ORDERS, THE BROWN TRASH BAGS HUNKER DOWN ON THE PATIO IN A COLUMN OF TWOS. A hard little caravan are they, resting in sunlight and shadow and caring not for their cargos, the sweepings of childhood and beyond.

With her eighteenth birthday near, Rachael has moved to Boston, leaving her room and the cleaning of it to us.

After conducting a one-family attempt at turning United Parcel Service into something resembling North American Van Lines, we gather by the front door early on a Sunday morning.

Beside the suitcases are stacked six boxes, taped and tied. In my innocence, I tap the topmost box and ask, "What are these?"

"That's the stuff I couldn't get in my suitcases last night; you guys can send it to me," she replies, rummaging through her purse. Out of habit, I begin a droning lecture on planning ahead, realize the futility of it, and am quiet.

She has a deep caring for the animals and purposely, we know, avoids saying good-bye to them, particularly the small female cat acquired during her stay at camp one summer, years ago.

The cat has shared her bed, has been her confidant and has greeted her in the afternoons when she returned from school. Good-bye would be too much, would bring overpowering tears, would destroy the blithe air of getting on with it she is trying hard to preserve.

We watch her walk across the apron of the Waterloo airport, clutching her ticket, and she disappears into the funny little Air Wisconsin plane.

Turning, just as she left the departure lounge, she grinned and flashed the peace sign. I was all right until then, but with that last insouciant gesture, so typical of her, the poignancy of the moment is driven home and tears come.

We hurry outside and stand in hot sunlight to see the plane leave. I note that we have never done this before, for anyone.

Clinging to the heavy fence wire along the airport boundary, I watch the plane take off to the west and make a last allegoric circle over Cedar Falls. East she travels and is gone, disappearing in the haze of an Iowa summer.

Back home, beer in hand, we sit on the porch, listening to the hickory nuts fall, recounting the failures and remembering the triumphs.

For the 500th time in the last eighteen years, we describe to each other the night of her birth, how she looked coming down the hall in the Bloomington, Indiana, hospital on the gurney in her mother's arms. How we felt, how we feel, what we did and didn't do.

We take a few days off, just to get used to the idea of there being only two of us again. Then, tentatively, we push open the door to her room.

The dogs peer into the darkness from around our legs and look up at us. The room—well—undulates. It stands as a shrine to questionable taste, a paean to the worst of American consumerism. The last few echoes of Def Leppard and Twisted Sister are barely audible. Georgia sighs.

I suggest flame throwers coupled with a front-end

loader and caution the cleanup crew, which now includes the two cats, about a presence over in one of the corners. Faintly, I can hear it rustle and snarl. It is, I propose, some furry guardian of teenage values, and it senses, correctly, that we are enemies.

Trash bags in hand, we start at the door and work inward, tough-minded.

"My god, look at this stuff; let's toss it all."

The first few hours are easy. Half-empty shampoo bottles go into the bags, along with three dozen hair curlers, four dozen dried-up ball-point pens and uncountable pictures of bare-chested young men with contorted faces clawing at strange-looking guitars.

Farther into the room salvage appears: the hammer that disappeared years ago; about six bucks in change; fifty percent of the family's towel and drinking-glass stock; five sets of keys to the Toyota. More. Good stuff. We work with a vengeance.

Moving down through the layers, though, we begin to undergo a transformation.

Slowly, we change from rough-and-tumble scavengers to gentle archaeologists. Perhaps it started when we reached the level of the dolls and stuffed animals. Maybe it was when I found "The Man Who Never Washed His Dishes," a morality play in a dozen or so pages, with her childhood scribblings in it.

In any case, tough-mindedness has turned to drippy sentimentality by the time we find the tack and one shoe from Bill, her horse.

I had demanded that Bill be sold when he was left unridden after the five years of an intense love affair with him were over. That was hard on her, I know. I begin to understand just how hard when Georgia discovers a bottle of horsefly repellent that she kept for her memories.

We hold up treasures and call to each other. "Look at

this, do you remember . . . ?"

And there's Barbie. And Barbie's clothes. And Barbie's camper in which the young female cat was given grand tours of the house, even though she would have preferred not to travel at all, thank you.

My ravings about the sexist glorification of middle-class values personified by Barbie seem stupid and hollow in retrospect, as I devilishly look at the cat and wonder if she still fits in the camper. "Here kitty, kitty. . . ." Ken is not in sight. Off working out on the Nautilus equipment, I suppose. Or studying tax shelters.

Ah, the long-handled net with which Iowa nearly was cleared of fireflies for a time. "I know they look pretty in the bottle, Sweetheart, but they will die if you keep them there all night."

Twister—The Game That Ties You Up in Knots. The ball glove. She was pretty decent at first base. And the violin. Jim Welch's school orchestra was one of the best parts of her growing years.

She smiles out at us from a homecoming picture, the night of her first real date. Thousands of rocks and seashells. The little weaving loom on which she fashioned pot holders for entire neighborhoods. My resolve is completely gone as I rescue Snoopy's pennant from the flapping jaws of a trash bag and set it to one side for keeping.

We are down to small keepsakes and jewelry. Georgia takes over, not trusting my eye for value, and sorts the precious from the junk, while I shuffle through old algebra papers.

Night after night, for a year, I sat with her at the kitchen table, failing to convince her of the beauty to be found in quadratic equations and other abstractions. I goaded her with Waller's Conjecture: "Life is a word problem." Blank stare.

Finally, trying to wave hope in the face of defeat, I

paraphrased Fran Lebowitz: "In the real world, there is no algebra."

She nodded, smiling, and laughed when I admitted that not once, in all my travels, had I ever calculated how long Smith would need to overtake Brown if Brown left three hours before Smith on a slower train. I told her I'd sit in the bar and wait for Smith's faster train.

That confirmed what she had heretofore only suspected—algebra is not needed for the abundant life, only fast trains and good whiskey. And, she was right, of course.

The job is nearly finished. All that remains is a bit of archiving.

I have strange feelings, though. Have we sorted carefully enough? Probably. Georgia is thorough about that kind of thing. Still, I walk to the road again and look at the pile. The tailings of one quarter of a life stacked up in three dozen bags. It seems like there ought to be more.

When I hear the garbage truck, I peer out of an upstairs window in her room. The garbage guys have seen lives strung out along road edges before and are not moved. The cruncher on the truck grinds hair curlers and Twister and junk jewelry and broken stuffed animals—and some small part of me.

She calls from Boston. A *job*. Clerking in a store, and she loves it. We are pleased and proud of her. She's under way.

The weeks go by. Letters. "I am learning to budget my money. I hate it. I want to be rich."

She starts her search for the Dream in a rooming house downtown and finds a Portuguese boyfriend, Tommy, who drums in a rock band and cooks Chinese for her. Ella Fitzgerald sings a free concert in the park. The cop on the beat knows her, and the store is crowded with returning college kids late in a Boston summer. Here in the woods, it's quieter now.

Her room has been turned into a den. A computer replaces curling irons and other clutter on her desk. My pinstripes look cheerless in her closet where pink fish-net tops and leather pants once hung.

Order has replaced life. I sit quietly there and hear the laughter, the crying, the reverberation of a million phone calls. The angst of her early-teen existential crisis lingers, drifting in a small cloud near the high ceiling.

And you know what I miss? Coming home and hearing her say, "Looking pretty good, Bob! Got your suspenders on?" She could make a whirring sound just like the motor drive on a fine camera.

Those few moments of irreverent hassle every day are what I miss most of all.

Regrets? A few. I wish I had walked in the woods more with her. I wish I had gotten mad less and laughed longer. Maybe we could have kept the horse another year.

Victories? A few. She loves the music and the animals. She understands romance and knows how to live a romantic life. She also has the rudimentary skills of a great blackjack dealer. I sent her off with that instead of luggage.

She has her own agenda. She's had it for years. It's not my agenda, not what I would choose, but then she has more courage than I do. She's out there on her own, cooking on a hot plate in a Boston rooming house, pushing and shoving and working and discovering. My respect for her escalates. She's going to be all right.

And I know I'll sit on the porch as autumn comes this year and other years, in some old sweater with some old dreams, and wonder where she goes and how she goes.

I hope she goes where there's laughter and romance,

and walks the streets of Bombay and leans out of Paris windows to touch falling January snow and swims in the seas off Bora Bora and makes love in Bangkok in the Montien Hotel.

I hope she plays blackjack all night in the Barbary Coast and, money ahead, watches the sun come up in Vegas. I hope she rides the big planes out of Africa and Jakarta and feels what it's like to turn for home just ahead of winter.

Go well, Rachael Elizabeth, my daughter. And, go knowing that your ball glove hangs on the wall beside mine, that Snoopy's pennant flies bravely in the old airs of your room, that the violin is safe, and that the little cat now sleeps with us at night but still sits on the porch railing in the late afternoon and looks for you.

Where the Wizard Lives

TIME IS MORE THAN ARITHMETIC, MORE THAN ADDITION AND SUBTRACTION AND THE ME-TERING OF YEARS AS THEY PASS. I have known this for a long while. Still, as the little car hums northward, I keep rolling the numbers over in my mind.

"Let's see, I'm 45. I was about 15 when I last walked the rivers. That makes it thirty years, certainly." "Not so," my intuition rumbles. It cannot be that long, not the three decades primly ladled out by the arithmetic. I consult my internal abacus, the one that reckons time by the clarity of images past. The answer whistles back immediately—less than thirty years, much less. Just as I thought.

Thanksgiving, 1984. Scott driving. Georgia, Martha, Rachael in the back seat. We are on our way to my mother's place in Rockford for the turkey, and, as it is when we are together, the air is rich with laughter and singing. Some of the humor is dark. "The banker takes the farm, the banker takes the farm, hi ho the dairy-o. . . ." And the day streams by in metaphor. Bright sun in Cedar Falls. Nashua washed in a curious high-mountain kind of yellow light flowing from a mixture of sun and clouds. By Rockford, grey overcast, wind.

This mission, a near-holy one for me, is more than a matter of meat and dressing. We're on our way to trace my boyhood paths along the Winnebago and Shell Rock rivers, to search the bottomlands for the old secrets, the ancient scents, and, most of all, to look for the place where the Wizard dwells, for it is there I began, and it is there that my ashes will scatter in a time yet to come.

> The last eagle rode the last wind of
>   summer,
> Blowing down the valley, as autumn
>   paid its call.
> I was walking by the river, listening to
>   the legends,
> Spoken by the meadow grass bending sweet
>   and tall.

The little safari begins on the west side of the Shell Rock, at the dam. Here, with a battered fly rod and small minnows, I did my best to decimate the school of crappies that, in spite of my efforts, replenished itself regularly. Across the way, by the old mill wall, the rock bass with their strange and beautiful orange eyes were found in the spring. In the riffles below, a smallmouth could be located now and then, and heavier tackle allowed a search for the big pike that washed down from the north in the spring floods. The day's take was hauled home, where my mother helped me do the cleaning under the back-porch light.

We walk slowly, and I am frustrated, chafing at my inability to recount everything, all of it. Language is linear, and the memories are not. The memories are images. Sunlight and current, the old mill at daybreak on Memorial Day, small bobbers going under as the crappies struck.

Images. My dad, waist-deep in the water, his nine-foot Calcutta bamboo rod bent from the pull of a big catfish 100 yards downstream as he whooped and cranked the star-drag reel. My mother, on evening expeditions, looking for flowers and pretty rocks along the bank.

Images. Old rowboats, old pipes, old tobacco. Books

we thought were racy then. The rise of the biggest bass you've ever seen late one October day. Images filtered through a lens of amber, made better than they ever were.

The railroad bridge. We have gotten that far now. If you listen closely, you can still hear the sound, feel the rumble, remember what it was like to dream of the road, when the Rock Island Rocket, a crack train too fast for the 'bos, bellowed across the trestle at 9:10 every night. I think of those lighted dining cars sometimes when I am heading east of Dubai at midnight on Air India 106, three hours this side of Bombay. And, reaching back like a mule skinner with his whip, I pull the memories forward.

Good memories. Old images. A country boy, with a fly rod and bucket full of minnows on a summer evening, looking up at the rails and wondering where the fast mail flew. Somewhere it went, out there, out beyond a world circumscribed by the distance you could walk and still be home for suppertime.

Up here on the grade, I am reassured. I can feel a slight vibration from downriver. The Wizard has remained, singing, rhyming out his lessons—"Watch the river and watch the fish, wet your finger and test the wind and make a wish. . . ."

I am laughing, pointing. Old trees that shaded me then. Sandbars. Clam shells. Deer sign. There is little evidence that boys still fish these places or dream of being riverboat captains on the Amazon. Other things now. Computers, I suppose. Things that appear less transient than the rivers and exude the warm illusion of providing for you in the future. It is likely that the fringe-benefit package for Amazon riverboat captains remains modest, at best.

> I guess I lay beneath every tree in
> Fischer's pasture,

Watching what the autumn does to
   leaves and butterflies,
Hearing ancient melodies and
   winnowing down the words
Of those who brought me promises and
   those who told me lies.

Farther down we go, and the Wizard's song is everywhere. We move through a small grove of trees. The sound of water against water is noticeable here. A few more steps and, before us, there is my place of growing and resting. The Shell Rock flows straight and true to the south. Coming in at a southeasterly angle, the Winnebago is momentarily thwarted by the strong current it must enter. Before the new dam on the Shell Rock was built twenty years ago, their merging was a seamless thing. Now the Winnebago fights for entrance, causing it to divide here at the end of its run. The result is a small and pleasant island, a wizard's tribute for the marriage rites.

We sit and are quiet. There is something about forever in this place. In the old times, we called it "the cutoff." Scott murmurs, "It is a place of magic. The Wizard does live here." Georgia, beside me, thinks of the task before her. It is she who must strew my ashes, and it is here she must do it.

I try to sort out the feelings. I am alive, breathing, healthy. Yet one day I will float out over these waters. Was it Camus who talked about the problem of conceiving of not conceiving? No matter. That is my struggle as I sit here on Thanksgiving Day, and the Wizard understands. He is just across the water, in the trunk of that old hollow tree. He lived there then, he lives there now.

After a while, we rise and begin to move up to the Winnebago; our quiet travels with us. This is a river with its own charms. Smaller and more mystical than the Shell Rock. It was easy for a boy to cross in the late afternoon, heading home with fish and a sense of things beyond the view of scholars and what passes for knowledge in schoolbooks.

My gift from the rivers was a simple one, but it took me a while to understand it. The universe will have me, as I had the bass, the bass had the minnows, and the minnows had the algae. When the great food chain is complete, all will be right, cash flows and income statements will not matter, computers will whir mindlessly, my guitars and flute will lie silent in their cases. But somewhere the music will live. That is my reason for all of this, and that is my comfort.

Up a bit from the cutoff, a little trickle of water enters the river from under thick brush on the west side. Behind that brush is a quiet pond. And beyond that one, another pond and yet another. It was in these ponds the wood ducks and mallards rested and fed until startled by the sloshing of water and a fly rod that poked through the bushes at them.

We move north, toward home, through timber less dense than it was. Dutch elm disease changed the face of Iowa. The contours are different. It is hard for me to find some of the old places. Without recognizing it, I pass by the stretch where the big smallmouth struck at the end of an autumn day.

For a moment, I am confused. The landmarks are gone. We are standing near a stubbled field, where the river bends. Looking up towards the town, I use the Methodist church steeple to orient myself. Ah, there used to be a red barn here and a meadow where horses grazed. I suddenly realize the walk has ended. We have covered the triangle on which a fair part of my younger days were spent. We are tired, windblown, cold, and the turkey waits.

My mother's house is warm and smells of November

cooking. I sprawl in a chair, stocking-footed, my Red Wings by the door. The years have not been wasted. Things have been accomplished. Yet I no longer have the feeling of time in my pocket and the weather on my side that I had then. I mourn the loss of that feeling, not of the years.

Someone mentions it is illegal for ashes to be scattered. Is it, really? I suppose it's true. Everything else has gotten more complex. Some biblical literalist, somewhere, roused from bureaucratic somnolence with a lurch and decided ashes to ashes is permissible, but ashes to water is not.

Still, the bottomlands and I were friends a long time ago. I think we shall be friends again, there in that place of four seasons turning, two rivers joining, and one wizard singing—singing some old song about fish and forever and fast trains in the nighttime.

Romance

*A speech delivered at the Summer Commencement ceremonies,
the University of Northern Iowa, Cedar Falls, Iowa.
July 29, 1983*

MR. PRESIDENT
MEMBERS OF THE PLATFORM PARTY
CANDIDATES FOR GRADUATION
FACULTY MEMBERS
PARENTS
LADIES AND GENTLEMEN

It seems more than just a bit strange to be standing here
today. It was in this very building, this room, that I received my B.A. degree in 1962. Prior to that event, however, I had spent an ungodly number of hours here in my
wildly misspent youth. You see, I played basketball for
what was then Iowa State Teachers College. For three
years I ran all over this room in short pants, dribbling and
shooting. I can still hear the voice of my late father as he
sat along the sidelines over there and shouted words of
encouragement as we battled the University of North Dakota or South Dakota State. He used to drive down from
Rockford, Iowa, on cold winter nights and add his voice
to the 4000 students who invariably packed this place as
we ran and jumped our way through season after season.
My father always thought books could make you happier
than basketballs. He was right. But that's another story
for another time.

The point is, this place is filled with memories, and memories play an important part in what I want to talk about today. Since I am Dean of the School of Business, I am absolutely sure a number of you turned out expecting to get some hot tips on microcomputer stocks or the latest news on money supply fluctuations. Sorry. Nor am I going to lecture you on (1) how well educated you are, (2) what wonderful opportunities you have before you, or (3) the importance of making great and lasting changes out there.

What I want to talk about is something a little different, something that makes all the living and doing you are so anxious to get on with worthwhile. More than that, it makes the living and doing better—better in terms of quality and quantity. I am going to talk about romance.

I looked up the definition of romance in several dictionaries. As I guessed, reading definitions of romance is about the most unromantic thing you can do. So I will not define romance, at least not directly. Rather, you will pick up a sense of what romance is by what I am going to say about it.

I am a musician and a writer of songs. One of my songs, which I call "High Plains Afternoon," starts like this:

> I see you now, as you were then,
> on a high plains afternoon.
> (Don't you remember the flowers,
> don't you remember the wind?)
> As naked you danced through the
> late autumn dust,
> while a threat of hard winter rode the cobalt horizon.
> (Don't you remember those who were free?
> We drove them out of our lives.)

As I sing the song, it carries a sense that I am singing

about a woman. Ostensibly I am. But it is also a song about the idea of romance, as she (pardon the gender) dances before us and then out of our lives, if we do not treat her right. Romance, you see, is something you have to take care of—romance needs food and water and care, of a kind all her own. You can destroy romance, or at least drive her away, almost without knowing that you are doing it. Let me give you an example.

A while back, a professor on this campus was finishing her doctorate. As part of her dissertation, she was conducting interviews with married folks about the subject of, well, marriage. When she asked Georgia Ann and me to participate, we thought it over. Then we politely said "no." Now, we have been married for almost twenty-two years, and a high level of zest remains in our relationship, so probably we have some useful things to say about marriage. Why did we decide not to? Because we have agreed that too much analysis of certain things removes the romance from them. Our relationship is one of those things.

Romance dances just beyond the firelight, in the corner of your eye. She does not like you to look at her directly; she flees from the cold light of logic and data collection when it is turned toward her. If you persist in trying to study her, however, she first disintegrates, then dissolves into nothing at all.

E. B. White once said a similar thing about humor, which "can be dissected, as a frog, but the thing dies in the process and the innards are discouraging to any but the pure scientific mind." You can't get at romance, then, by good old Western reductionism.

Understand, I am not just talking about romance in the sense of love between two people. You can't really have a romance with someone else unless you are, first of all, a romantic yourself. Most people I know are not very romantic. They were once, or had the chance to be, but romance got lost along the way, drowned in the roar of our times, beat out by overly analytic teachers, drummed out by those who scoff at romantics as foolish and weak. In those people, romance looked around and said, "I'm not living here; too cold."

What do romantics look like? You can't really generalize. Besides, to make a list of characteristics would be to commit the sin of breaking romance down into small pieces, which I cautioned about before. The best way to tell a romantic is to just be around one. You'll know. There is a sense of passion about them, a sense of living just a bit too far out at the edge emotionally, sometimes; a caring for what seem to be dumb things—an old chair you sat in during your graduate student days and in the early times of your career, a knife that lies on the desk year after year, a simple wooden box. You can tell a romantic by the voice—it dances because the mind is dancing.

And I can tell you this for sure: All romantics like dogs and cats, and maybe some other creatures, preferably animals that come in off the road for a little sustenance and decide to stay around and participate in the craziness they sense in this place of food and laughter. Animals like romantics, for they know they will never be let down by them.

It's important to note here that you do not have to be a poet or a painter or a musician to be a romantic. In fact, I know quite a few folks in these areas of endeavor who are downright unromantic. On the other hand, Andrew Carnegie was a romantic. So was Joseph Smith when he led the Mormons westward. And I have seen more than one insurance salesman, in the bars where I have played, grin outwardly and inwardly when I launched into a song about the wind and the flowers and the highways that run forever.

Robert Pirsig puts it well, in his book *Zen and the Art of Motorcycle Maintenance*, when he says, "The Buddha . . . resides quite as comfortably in the circuits of a digital computer or the gears of a cycle transmission as he does at the top of a mountain or in the petals of a flower. To think otherwise is to demean the Buddha—which is to demean oneself."

In a sense, romance is practical. It fuels your life and propels your work with a sense of vision, hope, and caring. Because you are working for others, not just for yourself, your work takes on a certain quality that it will not otherwise have. I suppose you can say romance puts meat on the table, though, as I say that, I feel more than just a slight drain on my system as romance prepares to leave.

Let me turn now to the matter of getting and keeping romance. Romance is hard to get, hard to keep, and fairly easy to drive away. If you are really intent on getting rid of romance, though, here are a few brief suggestions:

Become obsessive about neatness, particularly in the way your desk looks.

Install expensive shag carpet in your house, so that when the dog throws up or one of your friends spills a beer, all hell breaks loose.

Don't listen to any good music. Ignore Bach, Mozart, Pete Seeger, and the Paul Winter Consort. Instead, listen only to top-40 radio. This is a first-rate approach to giving romance a shove out of your life, for she likes subtlety and low decibel counts.

Excessive focus on detail and procedure at the expense of vision, of dreams, of reflection, is another good way to get rid of romance. We in the academic world have mastered this approach.

Buy birthday cards, anniversary cards, and the like instead of making up your own. All of us are poets; some have just lost their voices for a while. As Ray Bradbury once said, about people in general, "And they were all, when their souls grew warm, poets."

Finally, the surest way to lose romance forever is to do things just for money, even though your cells tell you this is not what you should be doing.

Now, in no particular order, here are some suggestions for keeping romance around you (or getting her back if she has flown):

Read some poetry every day. For starters, try a little Yeats, then some Kipling (along with some of his stories). I know Kipling must be terribly out of fashion nowadays, but romantics never concern themselves with fashion anyhow.

Set a new schedule for yourself and do your reading then. Try this: Instead of flopping around in bed, get up early—maybe 4 a.m.—on a Sunday, in the winter, when a classic Iowa howler is blowing in from the Dakotas. This works pretty well. Besides, you have the secret pleasure of being reasonably sure you are the only one in the Western Hemisphere reading Kipling at that very moment.

Here's another idea. Sometime in your life, build your own house or at least the most intimate parts of it. Design it, too, with lots of thought. You will get endless pleasure and romance from walking through doorways and knowing you put the door there with your mind and your hands.

Collect little things, like the old knife on your desk or the small box you had for keepsakes when you were a child. At a time in my life when I was just overcome with administrative burdens, and my face showed it, one of my faculty gave me a small wooden flute along with a note that said, "Don't let your muse slip away." I keep the flute where I can see it.

Play a musical instrument. Something you can get

out on those early mornings when reading is not the thing. Don't tell me you are not musical and, for heaven's sake, don't tell me you are tone deaf. I simply, if you'll pardon the expression, won't hear of it. If all else fails, or even if it doesn't, buy an Appalachian dulcimer. You can get warm, exotic sounds out of it right away without knowing anything formal about music at all. Try reading some ancient Chinese poetry while you strum the dulcimer. It works wonders.

Travel is good for romance. But don't just travel; *travel.* Here's what you need: notebooks, a small compass, a pocket atlas of the world, and a spyglass for looking out of airplane windows or across the rooftops of Paris or far down the country lanes in England. A word of warning is needed here: If you are traveling with your boss and he or she is not a romantic, be careful. You may not want to be seen with your compass and a spyglass on an airplane. If you are a true romantic, however, it won't matter much, because you will be good at what you do and your boss will just shake his or her head and mutter about what one has to put up with to get quality work these days.

Keep good journals of your life and travels. This is vitally important. I delight in reading and re-reading my adventures in the old markets of Saudia Arabia, where I bargained for gold and silver to bring home, and my wild ride through the streets of Riyadh late at night with a Bedouin cab driver who played Arabic music on a tape deck and tried to give me a short course in his language, while the best I could do was teach him to say "Kleenex" by pointing to a box of it on his dashboard.

I like knowing that I was in Richmond, Virginia, at 7:55 a.m. on June 7, 1981, or that I was in Paris in the snow in January 1982, or that I was once in Montego Bay, Jamaica, in the spring.

One of the most haunting entries in my journals

reads, "12:24 p.m. Back in Iowa Georgia and Rachael are sleeping (3:24 a.m.), and I'm over Egypt." When I wrote that, I remember feeling very far away, in more ways than just miles, somehow.

My secretary leaves me alone when I fall behind in an especially unappealing piece of work, and a cold, gray, November rain is splattering against the third-floor windows of Seerley Hall. She knows I'm traveling. I stand, put my hands in my pockets, stare out those windows, and I'm comforted by the knowledge that somewhere the big planes are turning for Bombay or Bangkok, for Brisbane or Barcelona, and romance is skipping along their wings.

But romance is not just outward bound. She also rides your shoulder when you turn for home, with your notebooks full, your suitcase packed with dirty clothes, when it's only a few days before Christmas and London's Heathrow Airport is pandemonium, with all flights overbooked. But then you're on, in your seat, London falls behind, Ireland is below; you get out the notebook again, and you write, "God, all I want now is to see Georgia, Rachael, the pups, Roadcat, and eat a giant plate of Georgia's world-famous spaghetti."

Finally, you've got to work at remembering that romance is all around you. It's not somewhere else. Here are two examples.

I had to go to the Hawaiian island of Oahu a while back. Everyone told me, before I went, how crass and junky Oahu and, particularly, Honolulu have become. It certainly looks that way, at first glance. "But," I said to myself, "romance must still be here somewhere." At first I couldn't see her. My vision was blocked by Don Ho standing around drinking a Pina Colada. But something caught my eye—and there was romance, right behind him, jumping up and down and waving to me. So, I got up before dawn, went down to the beach, rolled up my jeans, waded in, and stood there in the pre-dawn grayness, playing my flute with the water washing around me and thinking about what this must have looked like when Captain Cook first came around Diamond Head, his sails flapping in the trade winds. There were a few other people on the beach, but they paid me no mind; they were there for the same reasons. When I finished, I heard the sound of applause from a long way off. I turned; it was romance. I caught a glimpse of her, just as the first ray of morning sunlight struck the barrier reef while she danced along it. And, my notebook says, "Soft winds blow easy, here in the night time, as Oahu lies bathing in the sweet scent of orchids. This skyplane will ride the west wind to morning and land in L.A. just after dawn."

The second example has to do with Iowa. Iowa is a very romantic, mystical place. I can't explain it, but it's here. Anybody can see the Rocky Mountains—they're obvious. It takes a little more perspective to see the beauty of Iowa or the romance in the long sweep of North Dakota prairie west of Larimore. Once when I was working in the woods south of Wadena, in northeast Iowa, it started to snow late in the day. I worked on. As I did, I began to feel a presence. What was it? The woods were filling up with snow. What was there? It took me a moment, but then I knew: It was Iowa. Iowa, like romance, doesn't come up and pirouette before you, saying, "Hey, look, I'm beautiful." She just lies there, on hot June days, like a woman in the sun, while romance splashes around where the Winnebago runs to kiss the Shell Rock, just two miles below the place of my growing.

Well, that's enough. You get the idea. All I have left

for you is a test of sorts (you knew there would be a test, didn't you?). How are you going to know if you have lived the romantic life? Here's how. On your dying bed, after all the living and doing, you must run this poem by turn-of-the-century poet R. M. Rilke through your mind:

> I live my life in growing orbits,
> which move out over the things of this world.
> Perhaps I never can achieve the last,
> but that will be my attempt.
> I am circling around God,
> around the ancient tower,
> and I have been circling for a thousand years.
> And I still do not know,
> if I am a Falcon,
> or a storm,
> or a great song.

When you have done that, on your dying bed, if you can smile and nod quietly to yourself, you will have succeeded, and romance will ride your shoulder as you turn for home.

Go well. Remember the flowers. Remember the wind. Thank you.

The Boy from the Burma Hump

IN HIS APARTMENT IN CALCUTTA, THERE WAS A GRAND PIANO. He wore khaki then, walked the bazaars and tapped away at the piano or played lawn tennis during his leaves from upcountry. After a week or two, he was ready when the call came for the return to Dinjan.

He carried only a small suitcase for the journey, his "laundry" as he called it, and looked forward to getting back to the jungle and the mountains, away from the sterile and crumbling world of the British raj. His flight left Calcutta, climbing northeast over the Khasi Hills toward Assam, the secluded province that curls off main India and lies snuggled up on the left shoulder of Burma, just short of the Himalayan rise.

At Dinjan, he and the other pilots slept and took their meals in a large bungalow on the fringe of a tea plantation. Well before dawn, he was awakened by the hand of a servant boy. Now he stands drinking thick Indian tea on the veranda, looking out toward the jungle where leopards sometimes go.

An open four-wheel-drive command car arrives, and he rides through the heavy night toward an airfield five miles away. Time is important now, in this early morning of 1943. Since losing an airplane to Japanese fighters over the Ft. Hertz Valley, the pilots cross there only in darkness or bad weather when the fighters are grounded. He signs the cargo manifest, checks the weather report, and walks out to the plane.

Like delicate crystal, our liberties sometimes juggle in the hands of young men. Boys, really. Climbing to the top of the arch at the front of their lives, some of them flew into Asian darkness, across primitive spaces of the mind and the land, and came to terms with ancient fears the rest of us keep imperfectly at bay.

There was Steve Kusak. And poker-playing Roy Farrell from Texas. Saxophonist Al Mah, Einar "Micky" Mickelson, Jimmy Scoff, Casey Boyd, Hockswinder, Thorwaldson, Rosbert, Maupin, and the rest.

And there is Capt. Charlie Uban. Khaki shorts, no shirt, leather boots, tan pilot's cap over wavy blond hair, gloves for tightening the throttle lock. He waits in the darkness of northeast India for his clearance from air traffic control in nearby Chabua. There are perhaps a dozen planes out there in the night, some of them flying with only 500 feet of vertical separation.

Captain Charlie Uban. Twenty-two years old, 5 feet 9 inches, 141 pounds. Born in a room over the bank in Thompson, Iowa, when airplanes were still a curiosity and the long Atlantic haul was only a dream to Lindbergh.

Chabua gives him his slot, and he powers his C-47 down the blacktop through the jungle night, riding like the hood ornament on a diesel truck, with 5,000 pounds of small arms ammunition behind him in the cargo bay. He concentrates on the sound of the twin Pratt and Whitney engines working hard at 2,700 RPMs, ignoring the chatter in his earphones.

The plane, with its payload plus 800 gallons of gasoline, is two tons over its recommended gross flying weight of 24,000 pounds. Gently then, Charlie Uban eases back on the yoke, pulls the nose up, and climbs, not like an arrow, but rather in the way a great heron beats its way upward from a green backwater.

It gets dicey about here. If an engine fails, he does not yet have enough air speed for rudder control. And he's lost his runway, so there is no opportunity to chop the takeoff and get stopped. But he gains altitude, turns southeast from Dinjan, and flies toward that cordillera of the southern Himalayas called the Burma Hump.

His copilot and radio operator are both Chinese. In the next four hours, they will cross three of the great river valleys of the world: the Irrawaddy, the Salween, and the Mekong. In the place where India, Tibet, Burma, and Yunnan province of China all come together, the mountain ranges lining these rivers constitute the Hump.

This is the world of the China National Aviation Corporation (CNAC—pronounced "*see*-knack"). Jointly owned by China and Pan American Airways, CNAC flies as a private carrier under nominal military control of the U.S. Air Transport Command. In the flesh, CNAC is a strange collection of civilian pilots from the U.S., Australia, China, Great Britain, Canada, and Denmark.

They are soldiers of fortune, some of the best hired guns in the world at pushing early and elemental cargo planes where the planes don't want to go and where most pilots won't take them. As one observer put it: "All were motivated by a thirst for either money or adventure or both, and it was impossible to gain much of the first without acquiring a considerable amount of the latter."

Some were members of Claire Chennault's dashing American Volunteer Group—the Flying Tigers—mustered out of various branches of the U.S. military in 1941 to fly P-40 fighter planes with tiger teeth painted on the air coolers in defense of China. When the AVG was disbanded, sixteen of the remaining twenty-one Tigers decided to throw in with CNAC.

Dinjan is the penultimate stop, the last caravanserai,

on the World War II lend-lease column stretching from the United States to Kunming, China. Along sea and air routes to Calcutta, and then by rail to Dinjan, moves virtually everything needed to keep China in the war, including perfume and jewelry for Madame Chiang Kai-shek.

Japan controls the China coast and large slices of the interior. Until the spring of 1942, lend-lease supplies were shipped to Rangoon, freighted by rail up to Lashio, and moved from there by truck over the Burma Road to China.

Then Vinegar Joe Stilwell's armies, sabotaged by British disinterest in Burma and by the indecisive, factionalized, and corrupt government of Generalissimo Chiang Kai-shek, were driven north. With the Japanese owning Rangoon, the railhead at Lashio, and portions of the Road, China was closed to the outside by both land and water. So it fell to the pilots to ferry materiel from Dinjan to Kunming. To fly the Hump.

As he reaches higher altitudes, Charlie pulls on a shirt, chino pants, woolen coveralls, and a leather flight jacket. Going through 10,000 feet he switches over to oxygen. At 14,000 feet, he needs more power in the thin air and shifts the superchargers to high. Above the Hump now.

In summer, the monsoons force him to fly on instruments much of the time. With winter come southern winds reaching velocities of 100-150 miles per hour, and he crabs the plane 30 degrees off course just to counter the drift. Spring and fall bring unpredictable winds, frequent and violent thunderstorms, and severe icing conditions.

He will fly over long stretches where there is no radio contact with the ground, up there on his own, blowing around in the mountains without radar. "You had good weather information on your point of origin and your destination, and that was about it," he remembers. The

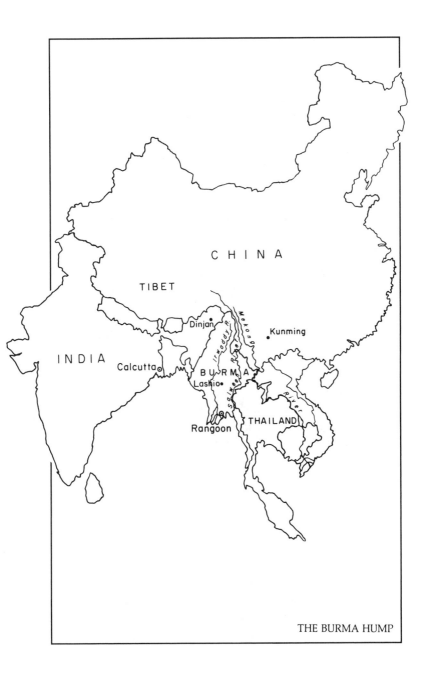

THE BURMA HUMP

primary instrument in use will be Charlie Uban's skills and instincts.

The winds push unwary or confused pilots steadily north into the higher peaks where planes regularly plow into the mountainsides. And there are other problems. Ground radio signals used to locate runways in rough weather have a tendency to bounce from the mountains. Even skilled and alert pilots mistakenly follow the echoes into cliffs.

Electrical equipment deteriorates from rapid changes between the cold of high altitudes and the tropical climate of Dinjan. Parts are in short supply, navigational aids faulty or nonexistent. But maintenance wizards do what they can to keep the planes rolling.

Pilots fly themselves into fatigue, sometimes making two round trips across the Hump in one day. Still they go, their efficiency and competence shaming the regular army pilots in the Air Transport Command. CNAC, with creative, flexible management and more experienced pilots, becomes the measure of performance for the entire ATC.

General Stilwell wrote in 1943: "The Air Transport Command record to date is pretty sad. CNAC has made them look like a bunch of amateurs." Edward V. Rickenbacker, chief of Eastern Airlines and America's ace fighter pilot in World War I, studies the situation, discounts all of the army's problems with airports, parts, and maintenance, and simply concludes that CNAC has better pilots.

Charlie Uban is paid $800 a month for the first sixty hours of flying. He gets about $7 per hour, in Indian rupees, for the next ten hours. For anything over seventy hours, he is on "gold," $20 per hour in American money.

A 100-hour month earns him roughly $9,000 in 1987 terms. The rare melding of technical competence, practiced skill, good judgment, and courage always pays top dollar, anywhere. The CNAC pilots chronicle their exploits by making up song verses using the melody to the "Wabash Cannonball":

> Oh the mountains they are rugged
> So the army boys all say.
> The army gets the medals,
> But see-knack gets the pay . . .

Not everyone can do it. They arrive as experienced flyers and are trained for the Hump by riding as copilots, committing the terrain to memory, absorbing the mercurial techniques of high mountain flying, and practicing letdowns in bad weather. There is no time for coddling. Those who can't move into a captain's seat in a few months are discharged. Charlie Uban got his command in three weeks.

One veteran pilot makes a single round trip as copilot, is terrified, and asks to be sent home by boat. Others will hang on, but are so intimidated by the Hump that they develop neuroses about it and become ill. Or, bent by their fears, they make critical mistakes where there is room for none. The Hump, rising out there in the darkness and the rain, is malevolence crowned.

Was Charlie Uban afraid? He thinks about the question for a moment, a long moment, and grins, "I'd say respectful rather than fearful."

Fear and magic sometimes danced together in northern Burma. A Chinese pilot was flying a new plane from Dinjan to Kunming. Over the middle of the Hump, the temperature gauge for one of the engines began climbing. The instructions were clear: "Feather the engine at 265 centigrade." Panic arrived at 250 degrees.

With a full load, a C-47 will fly at only 6,500 feet on one engine. So the choices were three. Feather the engine and descend to an altitude that is not high enough to get through the mountains, let the temperature escalate and burn up the engine, or bail out in the high mountains. Three alternatives, each with the same outcome.

But the manual had been written by Western minds. Therefore, and not surprisingly, the range of options was unnecessarily constrained. As the gauge hit 265, the pilot broke the glass covering the gauge and simply twisted the dial backwards to a reasonable level. Unable to get at the sender, he chose to throttle the messenger. There is some ancient rule at work here—if you can't repair the problem, at least you can improve your state of mind.

At Kunming, the gauge was diagnosed as faulty. The engine was just fine. Remember Kipling's famous epitaph? "Here lies a fool who tried to hustle the East." The C-47, like a lot of others, tried and failed.

If a crew goes down in the Hump region, no search party is sent. The territory is wild and rugged, settled sparsely by aboriginal tribes or occupied by the Japanese. The snow accumulates in places to a depth of several hundred feet, and a crashed plane just disappears, absorbed by the snow.

The pilots suffer through it and gather strength from one another, talking quietly when a plane is overdue and cataloging the optimistic possibilities. After a few weeks, the missing pilot's clothing is parceled out among the others and his personal effects are sent home.

Charles L. Sharp, Jr., operations manager for CNAC, is a realist. Roosevelt demands that China be supplied. There is not enough time for proper training. The weather is wretched, equipment humbled by the task, and the planes, which are cargo versions of the venerable DC-3s, always fly above the standard gross weight.

So lives are going to be taken. Sharp accepts that. Still, he grieves for the pilots who vanish out there in the snow or thunder into foggy mountains during letdowns in

China or blow up on the approach to Dinjan, and he worries about those who keep on flying.

Small samples from his logs in CNAC's war years intone a litany to risk and a chant of regret.

Aircraft No.	Captain	Date	Location	Crew
53	Fox	3/11/43	Hump	Lost
49	Welch	3/13/43	Hump	Lost
48	Anglin	8/11/43	Hump	Lost
72	Schroeder	10/13/43	Shot Down	Lost
59	Privensal	11/19/43	Kunming; let-down	Lost
63	Charville	11/19/43	Kunming; let-down	Lost

Between April 1942, when Hump operations started, and September 1945 at the end of the war, CNAC pilots will fly the Hump more than 20,000 times. They carry 50,000 tons of cargo into China and bring 25,000 tons back out. Twenty-five crews are lost. The consensus remains among those who understand flying that, given the conditions under which CNAC operated, the pilots were one of the most skilled groups ever assembled, the losses remarkably small.

Today Charlie Uban is freighting ammunition. Sometimes he carries 55-gallon barrels of high-octane gasoline, a cargo he prefers not to haul. Or he might be loaded with aircraft parts or medical supplies or brass fittings. Occasionally he moves Chinese bank notes printed in San Francisco and being forwarded to deal with China's sprinting inflation.

On his way back from Kunming, he will be dragging tin or wood or hog bristles, or mercury or silk or refined tungsten ore. Now and then he has a cargo of Chinese soldiers going to India for training. They are cold and airsick for most of the trip.

As Stilwell begins his 1944 push back down into the jungles of Burma, Charlie will haul bagged rice that is booted out of the cargo doors at low altitudes to construction crews following the armies. The crews are building a new land route, the Ledo Road, from India across northern Burma to China.

Conditions are seldom good enough for daydreaming. Most of the time he concentrates on his gauges and listens to the engines, ". . . envisioning misadventures and figuring out what to do about them ahead of time."

But now and then in clear weather he thinks about other things. He thinks about his girl, Emma Jo, back in Iowa and calculates the days left before he gets his three-month leave in the States. And he remembers Charles Lindbergh's solo flight across the Atlantic in 1927. He was six years old at that time, but somehow understood the magnitude of Lindbergh's achievement even then. That's what brought him here.

His family moved to Waterloo, Iowa, where he grew up building model airplanes and reading magazine articles about the new world of flight. At 15, he bicycled out to the old Canfield Airport and used $2 from his *Des Moines Register* paper route to purchase his first airplane ride on a Ford Trimotor.

Bouncing around in a single-engine Taylorcraft, Charlie Uban learned to fly at Iowa State Teachers College in 1940 as part of the federally sponsored Civilian Pilot Training program. At Iowa State College in Ames he studied engineering and passed the secondary stage of the CPT program. He learned cross-country techniques at a school in Des Moines, taught flying for a while in Aberdeen, South Dakota, and was trained as a copilot for Northwest Airlines in Minneapolis, where he picked up his instrument skills.

When Pan Am wrangled a contract for supplying the Far East, he went to work for them and flew as a copilot in four-engine DC-4s and C-87s, hauling cargo and passengers down the Caribbean to Brazil and from there to Accra on the coast of West Africa. In Accra, the cargo was off-loaded onto smaller planes for the flight over the desert and across Asia to Calcutta.

In the summer of 1943 he was riding copilot alongside Capt. Wesley Gray with a load earmarked for the Generalissimo himself. In Accra, they were ordered not to offload, but rather to continue on across Africa and Asia to Dinjan, pick up a Hump pilot to guide them through the mountains, and take the cargo on into Chungking.

On the way, Charlie bumped into a few CNAC pilots and talked with one of them at length. Since Pan Am owned 20 percent of CNAC, he applied for a transfer, and by the fall of 1943 he was flying the Hump.

The C-47 settles down on the runway at Kunming. It's 9 a.m. Charlie will spend the day at a hostel near the airfield. He will nap, play cards, and talk with other pilots. In late afternoon, he takes off for the westward flight back to Dinjan. Tomorrow he will fly the same route once again. Often he will make one-and-a-half, or even two, round trips in a single day.

Charlie Uban made 524 flights over the Hump in two years and knows of only one CNAC pilot who claims more wartime crossings. After the war, CNAC moved its operations to Shanghai. Charlie went along, flying all over the orient—north to Muckden in China, west to Calcutta, and south to Manilla.

Things got messy, though. Four planes crashed in one day in Shanghai due to weather and radio interference from commercial stations operating at illegally high power levels. The Chinese communists had begun firing on the CNAC planes, and there was dissension among the pilots over the way operations were being run.

Charlie had enough and came home to finish his mechanical engineering degree at Iowa State. He graduated in

1949 and entered the family oil business in Waterloo. In 1964, and again in 1968, he was elected to the Iowa legislature as a state representative.

The CNAC Alumni Association meetings are important to him. Friends come by. "I see Kusak and Norman there. It's an occasional refurbishing, a touching again . . . all the time, throughout the decades."

The old pilots talk about airplanes and mountains. Some flew for commercial airlines after the war or opened restaurants or farmed. Others, they say, smuggled gold through Asia and flew contraband in South America. There is a bond of forever among them. They bellied up against death, saw it all, and delivered the goods.

Any regrets about getting out of flying? Some. But Charlie Uban has looked backward, looked forward from there, and is comfortable with his choices. Yet he has a recurring dream in the nights of his life, even now. In the dream, he is flying low toward obstacles, trees and mountains and such, and there is never enough room to pass between them. He wonders about the dreams.

And I wonder what there is in the ordinary machinations of life to rival flying the Hump at twenty-two. Can the adrenalin ever flow that swift again? Can there ever be another sound as pure to the soul as the landing gear coming down at Kunming or a sight like that of Everest and Kanchenjunga to the northwest on a clear day as you come in to Dinjan?

Most of us think of life as a long upward sweep to some modest glory in our middle years. But if you have battled the great whale in your early times, what can ever compare? Maybe Hannibal or Lindbergh or the foot soldier at Normandy or even Orson Welles also suffered these proportions.

On the other hand, maybe none of this is important. Maybe it is enough to have done it and to live a life on the memories of having done it—of having swept upward from a thousand blacktop runways into the jungle nights on your way to China.

Others will do it again, but not in that place, in that way. The Hump, as a presence, has disappeared. It was a concoction of the times and the available technology. In a jet airplane, at 40,000 feet, the Hump no longer exists.

It's been forty-two years since Charlie Uban flew the Burma Hump. He talks about those times, late of an April afternoon, while Emma Jo makes supper noises in the kitchen. "I remember the time I realized I was doing an excellent job of flying this tough, tough route, and it just did wonders for my self-esteem." "If you're doing a good job, and somebody knows it and appreciates it, that's about as good as life gets."

His khaki uniform with a CNAC patch on the right shoulder drapes from the back of a chair. He wears a bush jacket from his India days and shuffles through piles of flight maps and logbooks and picture albums on the table in front of him. As he warms to the memories, his voice alternates between the past and the present tense, and he speaks softly, more to himself than anyone else, running a finger gently along his recollections.

"Fall of '43. Two of 'em crash in Suifu, up the Yangtze River from Chungking. Robertson is still up there in the overcast, sees two puffs of smoke come up through the clouds, decides that's enough of that, and heads back to Dinjan." "A hundred and twenty-one hours this month." "Here! Hydraulic pump failure, good weather, short of personnel; flying the Hump solo, no copilot, no radio operator."

"Kunming, Dinjan, Kunming, Kunming. That means I had trouble leaving Kunming and had to come back in." "Next day, blower failure and had to return." "Next day, the 14th, rice dropping." "January 6, 1945, Russ Coldron disappears over the Hump." "January 7, 1945, my old friend Fuzzy Ball flew into Tali Mountain. . . ."

His voice trails off to a murmur as he reads. From his kitchen table in Iowa, Charlie Uban is reaching back four decades into the night and the wind and the deep snows of the southern Himalayas where some of his friends still lie.

I listen not so much to the words themselves, but rather to the sound of his memories. It's something like the drone of a C-47 cruising out there east of Dinjan, above the Burma Hump, in the days when it was pretty clear who was right and who was wrong. Over his shoulder I can see airplanes coming and going at the Waterloo Airport a mile away.

Just outside the window, wood ducks are circling among the trees by a pond, peering through the fog at the end of a rainy afternoon, looking for a place to land. Captain Charlie Uban watches the lead drake come in through the dusk on his final approach, sees him catch the headwind as he lets down through the haze, and nods his appreciation—from one old pilot to another.

Whether it's Dinjan or Calcutta, Kunming or Shanghai, or a small pond in Iowa, those who live on the wing understand one another. They have been taken aside by Iris, trained by scholars of the twilight. And, while the rest of us plead for guidance and struggle for the trace, old fliers have no need of that, for they know secret things and hear distant ragas that carry them along the great bend of the night toward home.

Leonard

LEONARD STILL COMES BY THE OFFICE ONCE OR TWICE A WEEK. We sit as old friends now, drinking coffee, while the late-autumn sunlight slants through the high west windows of Seerley Hall. Perched on the edge of his chair, hunched over with intensity, he unravels the latest in his never-ending stream of ideas about how the school, and the world in general, can be improved. He is still tall and raw-boned, but he hasn't felt so good lately. The doctor says there is something inside of him, something that is nasty and growing. Not much time left, so the judgment goes.

I first met Leonard when I came down out of the flat country north of Cedar Falls. I had a pretty fair twenty-foot jump shot and not much else, except some dreams I couldn't articulate. Leonard came over to the basketball games, talked to me in the halls, and encouraged me to sign up for a few of his marketing courses.

Those were the old days. Sometimes he taught six courses a semester, lecturing for eighteen hours a week. He grumbled about the load, without ever sounding like he was really complaining, and told us if we were taking more than one or two of his courses, it would be redundant, since he couldn't possibly prepare eighteen different lectures each week. He was right.

But, somehow, we didn't care. He was falsely gruff, entertaining, and he loved us all. It was Advanced Living

402, not marketing, and we knew it.

I graduated and entered the Air Force. I seem to remember Leonard even had a hand in that decision. After a while, though, an allergy surfaced that prevented me from doing what the Air Force wanted done, and a medical discharge was provided.

Drifting, I stopped in Cedar Falls to visit old friends, especially Leonard. He said if I wanted to enroll in graduate school, he would design a special program for me that avoided the crap. He did.

Over the next year-and-a-half, I studied hard for a change, mostly in private tutorials with Leonard and in courses he selected for me. One day he called me at my old apartment and said a fellow from Indiana University's Graduate School of Business was in town recruiting students for M.B.A. study. Leonard suggested I come up and talk about going on for a doctorate at Indiana. Wait a minute! That was the sort of thing other people did, people from the east coast or Iowa City, not kids with now-fading jump shots from Rockford, Iowa. I had never even seen a professor before I went to college, and here this guy, Leonard, was nudging me toward being one.

The Indiana professor only had M.B.A. application forms with him. Leonard said something to the effect that, "Hell, they're all the same," crossed out "M.B.A." and wrote "Doctorate" in its place. I filled out the form, took the Admission Test for Graduate Study in Business in Cedar Rapids, and forgot about it. In April, the people at Indiana called to say I had been accepted. I went to Leonard's office in the basement of Sabin Hall. He organized a small celebration and had tears in his eyes. Leonard never got his Ph.D. He came right from the business world to teach and, in spite of his lack of credentials, managed to become a full professor. Not many did, or do, that.

"I have the best damn job in the State of Iowa, maybe the world," he used to tell me. I couldn't quite see how that was true at the time, but I took it as an article of faith and trundled off to Bloomington in search of higher things.

During the first couple of years in Indiana's grinding program, Leonard wrote me letters of encouragement. Along about the third year, he changed tactics and started a campaign designed to persuade me to return after I finished my doctorate. He knew, as I found out, that prestigious universities do not look fondly upon their illustrious graduates going on to teaching positions in small, out-of-the-way schools. The gentle prodding of his letters was all but drowned in the precisely enunciated litany intoned by my dissertation advisor: "Berkeley, Berkeley, Berkeley."

After my daughter was born, Leonard intensified his crusade and switched his letter writing to her, with patently sham marketing techniques designed to convince her two-month-old mind that life was good in Cedar Falls and that her father would enjoy teaching at what had become the University of Northern Iowa. Only Leonard, because of who he is, can get away with such nonsense. He not only gets away with it, he makes it work.

I came back. Several of us formed a new department with about 100 students and started to build a business program. Leonard was the first department head. He tried it for three years, hated it, and returned to the classroom. We grew, changed, developed. Leonard led the charge, out in front of us all, cajoling, arguing, stroking, berating, and never quitting. Now when he comes by, we talk about the problems of managing an organization that has grown to almost sixty faculty members and 2,700 students, along with graduate programs, consulting operations, centers, and the rest.

Last week, the local chapter of the American Marketing Association gave Leonard an award for his long and dedicated service. In his talk to the assembled faculty and students, he said, "You're as good as any person in the U.S. . . . better than the majority of them. I've had a terrific job and the best life of anyone in Iowa, and I've had the privilege of being associated with over 10,000 students." There he is, twenty-five years later, telling them the same things he told me and meaning it just as much as he did back then.

Leonard's former students always have kept in touch with him. The mail and phone calls, though, have picked up as word gets around about his illness. An ex-quarterback who became president of a large investment corporation in California writes to say hello. The director of the Harvard M.B.A. program does the same. One person calls him one week, another person the next.

What is there about Leonard Keefe that makes us love him so? Well, I can't put it any better than I did a few years back when I had the honor of presenting him with an outstanding teaching award just before his retirement: "Leonard's real gift is in taking us country boys and girls and making us believe we can do more than we ever thought we could do."

He still makes us believe here in these latter times, as he marches along in his yellow windbreaker, hiding the pain, covering the fear. And behind him, in the dust, we march—his private alumni army, 10,000 of us, trying to be just half as good as Leonard is on his worst days.

Ridin' Along in Safety
with Kennedy and Kuralt

INDIANA AUTUMN. Bloomington, in 1967. The man comes through little swinging doors separating the dining room from the bar in the Holiday Inn. He smiles and asks, "Do you boys know the 'Wabash Cannonball?' " I do, but I haven't done it for a while. My partner, Wayne Schuman, riffles around on the 5-string banjo for a moment, grins his funny little grin, nods to me. "Yeah, we can get through it," I say. The man and some friends are eating in the dining room and can hear the music just fine through the doorway. Back he goes to his table, carrying a napkin.

Wayne and I crank it up—"From the green Atlantic Ocean to the wide Pacific shore. . . ." I'm singing and playing the guitar, Wayne is flying along behind me, working out his instrumental break as he backs me up. "This train, she rolls through Memphis, Mattoon, and Mexico. . . ." It's early. The bar is only a third full as we hit the chorus: "Listen to the jingle, the rumble, and the roar, as she glides along the woodlands, through the hills, and by the shore. Hear the mighty rush of engine, hear the lonesome hobo call. Ridin' along in safety on the Wabash Cannonball." We end and look at each other. Not bad for the first time through the tune together.

Back the man comes, through the swinging doors. Three others are with him. A round, familiar-looking fellow with friendly eyes asks if we'll play the song one more time. Playing the bars over the years has prepared me for things worse than singing a song twice in a row, so we do it.

After we finish, the round fellow holds out his hand. "I'm Charles Kuralt from CBS. We're doing a television piece on the death of the Wabash Cannonball, and we want you boys to play the music for it, right here in the bar." Confusion takes over. The motel manager is gone. The bartender, Cliff, is a suspicious sort, as bartenders are wont to be. This is his world, he's responsible for it. Finally, he agrees that Kuralt and his crew can do what they want, as long as nothing is damaged.

Confusion turns to chaos. Kuralt's old van is pulled up to the outside door of the bar. People are carrying lights, cameras, sound equipment. While this is going on, Kuralt interviews us. I'm writing my doctoral dissertation and playing here on weekends, trying to get my wife, baby daughter, and myself through the last year of an interminable number of years of school. Wayne is an undergraduate, playing mostly for fun.

People in the bar are agog, asking questions. We announce over the mike what is taking place. This leads to a crush at the pay phone in the lobby as they call friends ("Yes, yes, CBS Television is going to film the folksingers right here in the Holiday Inn bar."). Five minutes later cars start screeching into the motel parking lot. The friends are arriving. Chaos shifts to pandemonium. Cliff is mixing drinks at record pace, while the waitresses fight their way around equipment, over cords, and through people streaming in and about the bar.

Forty-five minutes go by; Kuralt's crew is ready. Sound test. Okay. The klieg lights come on; it looks like mid-day in what was a dark bar. The labels on the two big cameras in front of me say "CBS TELEVISION." "Jeez, this is for real," I think. The sound man lies on the floor at my feet, just out of view of the cameras, holding a large microphone that looks like it means business.

"All right," someone says, "start playing and don't stop until we tell you to." Sweaty hands. "Here's to Daddy Claxton, may his name forever stand. . . ." Ten minutes later they flag down the Cannonball. Next, we do just the banjo part for six or seven minutes, Wayne's magical, double-jointed right hand waving like long grass in the summer wind as he picks.

It's over. "Yeah, thanks, we enjoyed it too." We take a long break. Cliff counts receipts and mumbles about "city folks." We stagger through the rest of the night, continually rejecting requests to play the "Wabash Cannonball" one more time.

A few days later, TV on, and Cronkite smiles, "Here's a report from Charles Kuralt, who's on the road." There we are! We're on the screen for about a minute, hammering away, with some voice-over by Kuralt about the end of the Cannonball (he's riding on the last run). Kuralt interviews passengers and the conductor. At the end, an aerial view shows the train moving away, whistle blowing. They have synched the guitar and banjo with the clicking of the wheels. It's pretty touching. She fades into the distance, almost out of sight, and Kuralt says softly, "Tomorrow the Wabash Cannonball won't be a train at all, only a banjo tune."

Cronkite sighs, "That's the way it is. . . ." My phone rings. It's an old friend from Connecticut, shouting. "I can't believe it! I just saw you on Walter Cronkite." We talk. I hang up, and the phone rings again. Everybody in the world watched Cronkite tonight. They run the tape the next day on a morning news show, then later on a program called "The Best of Charles Kuralt." We're famous, sort of.

A few months later the phone rings once again. A breathless voice asks if he's talking to the guy who did the Cannonball thing for Kuralt. Yes. He's from Robert Kennedy's campaign headquarters. The Senator saw the show and wants us to go with him on an old-fashioned whistle stop tour in Indiana, for which they'll take the Cannonball out of retirement. Will we go? Yes, but it will cost $200. He doesn't care what it costs. (I curse my inexperience.)

Small town in north Indiana. April 1968. On the train with journalists, TV crews, and lots of other people in nice suits just running around. We are instructed to report to the last car, the Kennedy car. Bobby, Ethel, kids, dog. They need publicity shots. Sixteen (I counted) cameras from around the world zoom in on the Senator, Wayne, and me—"Listen to the jingle, the rumble and the roar. . . ."

First stop. Secret Service types lead us onto the back platform, guns visible when they turn just right. Bobby and Ethel follow them, then us. The Senator holds the mike for me. ". . . as she climbs along the woodlands, through the hills and by the shore." Thousands of people, screaming, holding up signs for and against the Kennedy effort, pushing to get close to the platform. Men with cameras on their shoulders are fighting the crowd and trying to get a foothold on the slippery rails.

We go on, from town to town. The scene repeats itself. Guns, crowds surging, Bobby talking in his persuasive way about problems and people. He holds the mike for me as we pull away. "Ridin' along in safety on the Wabash Cannonball."

Back in Iowa, I receive the check from Kennedy campaign headquarters the morning he is shot. Strange. Probabilities. I somberly walk to the bank and cash it. Strange.

Bobby Kennedy is dead, Charles Kuralt is still on the road, and Wayne Schuman doesn't play anymore. I get out the old Martin guitar, late in the day, and once in a while I quietly sing, "Listen to the jingle. . . ." Once in a while.

Going Soft upon the Land

Going Soft upon the Land and Down along the Rivers

Then he was told:
Remember what you have seen
because everything forgotten
returns to the circling winds.
—NAVAJO WIND CHANT

OLD MEN AND OLD RIVERS—IT'S GRAVITY THAT DOES THEM BOTH IN. That being so, I have come to the river again before gravity tugs too fiercely upon the pocket of my jeans. I have come to ride the water of my growing years and to wonder about Iowa, about where we go and how we get there, and whether we might do more than just adapt and endure. I have returned to ask why it is we are less than we might have become.

There is a sense of having lost our way, as a state and as a nation. Yet within the reach of this curious place called Iowa is a chance to show the way to those who have lost it. I will think about that by the meadows and along the cliffs of my river.

And I have come to test a proposition from the writings of Albert Camus. He once said, ". . . a man's work is nothing but a long journey to recover through the detours of art the two or three simple and great images which first gained access to his heart." Out here where the river runs and those images formed, I first began my search for the secret places where magic and fire and the cold edge of reason interlace. I have come to extend the search; I have come to look for Iowa.

So it is that on a candy-striped dawn in late summer I am bent over my canoe ten feet below a small dam in southern Minnesota. On the southeast curve of Albert Lea Lake, water flows south through an outlet twenty feet wide, passes under a bridge on a county road, and forms a small pond behind the dam. The Shell Rock River begins here.

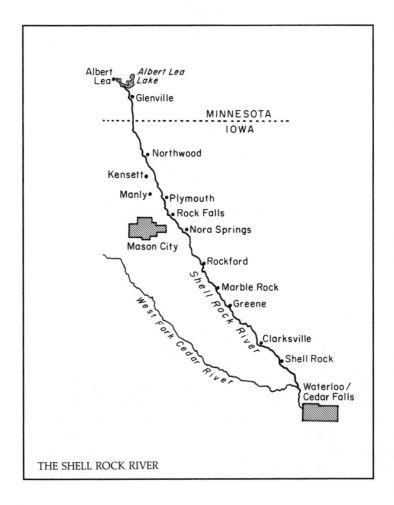

THE SHELL ROCK RIVER

With bowline knots I lash my river bag and tent to the ashen stern thwarts of the little boat. A five-gallon water container and camera tripod go in toward the bow, the spare paddle is wedged between the river bag and the gentle camber of the hull. She is trimmed to fly and I am ready.

Straightening up, I look downriver from underneath my hat brim, squinting hard through new light. Cedar Falls looks like a long way from here. I estimate the distance at 115 river miles, 100,000 paddle strokes. But thinking about it won't get me there, so I push off in shallow water, paddling easily down what the American Indians called "Neshonagaton," Otter River. Paddling toward Iowa, at the turn of my 47th year.

Morning music plays somewhere in the back of my head. A guitar and flute. I hum along without thinking about it, stroking in time with the meter of the song.

As I round the first bend, a blue heron lifts from her place along the shore, indolently beating her way southward. For nearly seven days on the river she will always be just in front of me, watching the water, watching me, and seeing through us both. With her about, I am glad I am not a fish, though sometimes I have thought I might like to be one.

Like some great hunter of old, she knows the territory, sighs at the intrusion, and understands the sooner she gets the pilgrim through, the sooner the shores and trees will once more be hers. She has seen other travelers. Some were wrapped in fur and came walking the far land bridges from Asia. Some floated these waters in boats of skin; others were mounted on fast ponies moving westerly through long bluestem grass.

I am a little uneasy, though. The Shell Rock is having trouble deciding whether or not it really wants to be a river. The land seems to resent the audacity of the water's challenge and tries to stand firm against the hard press of current. I make my way around long curves and through bayous filled with mallards, wondering if it all will come to a halt in a muddle of fallen trees and waving swamp grass.

The path is nearly blocked at one point by tangled limbs, but I slip through a small opening where the river flows westward, navigate a bend, and swing south. A choice has been made. The land yields, banks form, and the river pushes on toward Iowa.

Here in the north, the river reminds me of canals I have seen in the French countryside. Flat and smooth, about forty feet wide, grassy banks all green and gold in the morning sun. Beavers swim in and out of the tall grass by the shore and warn each other of my coming with soft "splats" of tails on water. But the canoe moves so silently that sometimes I pass within five feet of them, unnoticed.

I slide under Freeborn County, Minnesota, Bridge #24518, constructed in 1978 so the metal plaque says, and move toward Glenville. The only sound is the soft gurgle of my wake when I turn, as the pointed bow searches for the channels.

Some evidence exists that "canoa," meaning "boat made from single timber," is the first American word that passed into the European language. I'm not surprised, since the forerunners of my canoe likely were the first objects Columbus's fleet saw as it approached the New World. Mine is a We-No-Nah Solitude. A solo canoe, small by normal standards. Fifteen feet six inches long and only $27^1/_2$ inches maximum width at the gunnels. Thirty-five pounds and colored light blue, like the sky above me.

The Solitude's parent was a marathon racer. It is fast and fairly maneuverable: A boat for small streams. It does not forgive incompetence easily, however, and some find it uncomfortably tippy. That's the price you pay for other qualities.

Good design is all whether you're fashioning a life or building a canoe. An interesting fellow named George Dyson once talked about building boats by saying, ". . . you start with a slender form the wind and the waves won't notice." I think his basic design principle can be generalized somewhat beyond boating.

Early in the day, except for lampposts and pavement, the main street of Glenville looks like something out of a John Ford western. If you squinch your eyes just right, you can see riders in long coats and Stetsons along the flat, spare street. I don't linger, though. For reasons I have no need to explore, this has the fume of alien territory, and something undefined nudges me toward the Iowa border.

Maybe it was a premonition, for trouble starts just below Glenville. The river is badly silted in this stretch, so I have only about ten inches of water under me. This involves shallow strokes and makes controlling the boat difficult. But that's not the main problem.

The problem is wire—wire across the river. Some of it is barbed, some electric. By the time this vulgar custom of fencing in the river dribbles out near Plymouth, Iowa, I will have had to deal with twenty or so different strands.

Some of the wire is rusty and in bad repair. But it remains in place to destroy the sense of a river running free. Some of it is charged, unreasonably and probably illegally, by 110 household current, and I take a terrific jolt at one crossing. On another occasion it almost causes me to capsize as I come down a long, fast rapids and cannot see the wire strung in the shadows of a bridge.

If the wire is just high enough, I can lie back on the river bag behind me and float beneath it. Other times I cross on the shore and pull the canoe under it with the bow painter.

I am angry about the wire. Aside from the hazards of shock and the inconvenience of circumventing it, the wire simply spoils the river. Like pesticides in drinking water or smoke from a factory or noise from a neighbor's stereo, the wire is an example of what economists call "externalities"—somebody's way of generating revenues becomes someone else's cost, even though the second person is not sharing in the revenues.

There must be better ways to design cattle ranges and containment. Not just for scenic virtues and canoeists. That would be a little too prissy, perhaps, though probably reason enough. More importantly, this approach to fencing leads to a degradation of riverbank integrity, since it allows our beefy friends to stomp and churn, not to mention defecate, along the shore and in the water. The results are silting, muddy water, and pollution. Some invention is needed. Meanwhile, I can only apologize to the river and the land for the indignity they jointly suffer.

Heading southwest, I go under a Highway 65 bridge in late morning. After fighting my way through more wire near the bridge, I drift a few hundred yards downstream around a bend and stop for lunch. In a pretty little grove on the west bank, a Granny Smith apple, some trail mix, a rice cake, and a chocolate bar set things right.

In the early afternoon, I am still moving through shallow water, around and under wire, and beginning to notice the heat. My pocket thermometer indicates it's over 90 degrees Fahrenheit. With deportment impeccable, I pass Judicial Drainage Ditch #20.

Just after Goose Creek has joined the Shell Rock, I round a bend and spot a pair of white pelicans enjoying the serenity of a summer river. They are shy, but not skittish, watching me carefully. I float by, clicking away with my camera, and they paddle north out of sight. White pelicans, on a quiet river, in Hartland township, Minnesota.

In spite of my excitement over seeing the pelicans, the airiness of spirit I felt at dawn has vanished, the music is faint. This is a world of hard sun and low water, and I am making only about two miles per hour. Even though I have prepared for this trip, my back is hurting, and the heat is nearly intolerable.

Water reflects about 80 percent of the sunlight hitting it, so with the temperature well over 90 and a clear blue sky, the river has become a formidable place, particularly when you are sitting only a foot or two above it. Even the flock of eighteen Canadian geese seems reluctant to fly as I move closer. Finally they rise, complaining loudly, quickly gather into formation, and head upriver.

By three o'clock I am looking for a campsite. At four, I find it. The Shell Rock, which has been flowing east for about a mile, runs into a high bank and turns south once more. On the outside of this curve is a pleasant sandy beach, and a few yards up from the beach is a small stand of bur oak and river willow. It looks promising from the water. Letting the current do most of the work, I use my paddle as a rudder, turn the bow upstream, and the canoe crunches gently up against the sand.

A quick survey of the place confirms my judgment from the river. Except for a fair supply of mosquitoes, this will do nicely. In an hour the tent is up and the gear organized.

After supper, there is time for writing in my journal and speculations about my location. It strikes me that I really don't know where I am, since the only map I have is a very rough mental one. Northwood, Iowa, is somewhere below, that's clear. How far, I have no sense. My best guess is that I am just about smack on the Iowa-Minnesota border.

I sit before a small camp fire and watch huge storms moving up in the west. There is fire in the sky, on the ground before me, and I remember that my own respiration is a form of combustion. Things get elemental out here. It's easy to forget the basics, and I believe such forgetfulness is at the heart of much of what afflicts our contemporary world. We have become so far removed from our natural systems that we take them for granted. They are just out there and are *supposed* to be there as a kind of supply dump and waste repository. I think we're about to hear nature's wail of neglect.

The lightning is as savage as I can ever recall. I retrieve some rope from the canoe and add extra tiedowns to the tent, front and back. But the worst of it goes north of me, so I am left with an easy rain and my thoughts about the river.

Old rivers and young people sometimes form strong bonds with one another. That's what happened in my case. When I was growing, the Shell Rock flowed clear and fast. It was only a block or so away from my home in Rockford and was a source of incredible variety for me. I spent my days along and on and in it. At the end of a summer day, the stringers were almost always heavy as I walked through the twilight toward home.

The Wizard lives along the river's banks. I lay upon my back in the evening pastures below Rockford and listened to him. That was forty years ago. His words were ministerial, and he gently prodded—"Watch the river and watch the fish, wet your finger and test the wind and make a wish." So I would listen, and laugh as he jumped and ran in ever-growing circles, tracing rings around the moon. And he created within me, in the words of Thomas Wolfe, ". . . a passionate and obscure hunger for voyages."

By the time I was in high school, there were other enticements. I went to the river less frequently. But when I did, I noticed strange things. There were fish, game fish, bloated and floating belly-up with sores on them. Carp, unbothered by the foulness, came snuffling in and dominated.

And the river of otters began to die an ugly death. By the late 1970s, people along the northern part of the Shell Rock had to keep their windows closed. The stench from the water was that bad. When the wind was right, the river could be smelled a mile away.

You could have dragged a minnow seine all the way from Albert Lea to Northwood and come up empty. Studies showed the river was devoid of both oxygen and fish for that fifteen-mile stretch, and, of course, the effects were felt much further downstream as well.

The same data clearly indicated that the major culprits in all of this were the city of Albert Lea and the Wilson packing plant located there. Unbelievably, the waste discharge from Albert Lea constituted 65 percent of the total flow of the river at the Albert Lea Lake outfall. Albert Lea turned the handle and everything unmentionable in polite company and family newspapers flushed down the Shell Rock.

It worked like this. The higher forms of life in a stream are aerobic; they need oxygen for survival. Healthy water contains oxygen in dissolved form that supports aquatic life. As the sewage load from Albert Lea hit the river, bacteria in the stream began their job of feeding on the wastes and breaking them down. The bacteria require oxygen to carry out this aerobic degradation.

The dissolved oxygen in water is replenished by reoxygenation at the air-water interface and also by photosynthesis activity of water plants. But if the waste load is heavy enough, the oxygen consumed by the bacteria engaged in degradation exceeds the replenishment process, and the amount of dissolved oxygen in the stream sags. If the sag is great enough, fish die.

A 1970 study of the river showed that the level of dissolved oxygen was too low to support most game fish all the way down to Nora Springs. Even rough fish could not exist in the upper reaches of the river. The sag had become a permanent valley.

As a sewage load becomes greater and greater, aerobic degradation cannot handle the job. Bacteria that do not use free oxygen, but rather use organically or inorganically bound oxygen from such common sources as nitrates and sulfates, continue the task. Gaseous by-products result that cause a river or lake to smell.

By 1978, the Iowa State Hygenic Laboratory drearily concluded that "The Shell Rock River, once rated as a highly productive and desirable aquatic resource, will remain one of the worst examples of water quality in Iowa until the quality of the water received from Minnesota improves."

The mess in the river was exceeded only by the behavior of those supposedly responsible for dealing with the problem. Albert Lea whined about the lack of money to build a new sewage treatment plant. Wilson balked during negotiations over what share of the cost it would pay.

Congressman Tom Hagedorn of Minnesota said he didn't really see what could be done. The water quality control commissions of the two states were not in communication with one another. In Iowa, the *Des Moines Register* tracked this inanity and, on July 2, 1978, ran a desperate headline: "Two states don't talk as stream dies."

Albert Lea received a federal grant to begin work on the lake, the source of the Shell Rock. But that money was used, instead, to clean up a nearby residential lake bordered by some of the finer homes in the city and the Albert Lea Country Club.

Meanwhile, this old river, the river of pike and bass,

of catfish and beaver, of mussels and muskrats, staggered and fell to its knees. And far downstream, if you listened closely, you could hear a sad song late in the night. The Wizard looked at the dying river and did not comprehend. His was the alchemy of fish and frogs and willows growing in a circular stand.

From an aesthetic, recreational, and even spiritual point of view, the situation was unforgivable. Yet from another perspective it was quite understandable, for the circumstances surrounding the debasement of the Shell Rock stand as a metaphor, of sorts, for many of our contemporary problems.

Consider the dilemma of chlorofluorocarbons and their insidious impact on the ozone layer in the earth's stratosphere, a layer that provides us with protection from excessive doses of ultraviolet radiation. If Sherwood Roland's theory, which he first proposed in 1974, is correct, and there is increasing evidence to support him, we are doing considerable damage to the ozone layer through our use of air conditioning, refrigeration, plastic foam packaging, and other products containing chlorofluorocarbons.

Why don't we stop it? Why didn't Albert Lea stop polluting the Shell Rock when it became obvious that great damage was being done? The city was using Albert Lea Lake, and hence the river, as a sink for its sewage, just as manufacturing firms and consumers in the United States and abroad are using the air as a sink for chlorofluorocarbons. In both cases, people are benefiting by externalizing part of the costs of their production or usage onto someone else. That "someone" often happens to be the natural environment.

If the river had been owned by a person, or, better yet, *was a person*, howls of protest accompanied by lawsuits immediately would have appeared. But the river was not private property; it was owned collectively by all of us. Not just Iowans, but everybody. Collective ownership of such a public commodity is often dispersed, as it is in the case of the river and the air, rather than concentrated as in the case of a private commodity. You can rob the river but not the banks, in a manner of speaking, where the pun is intended.

It came down to a decision problem. Albert Lea was faced with two choices. One was to build the sewage plant. The second was to maintain the status quo. From the city's point of view, the lake was already dead and building the plant would not revive it. The river? That was downstream and was not bothering Albert Lea. Iowans would enjoy all the benefits of a new plant, would ride free on the backs of Albert Lea's expenditures.

So the first alternative involved punishment in the form of costs. The second alternative's outcomes appeared cost free. Confronted with such a decision, what does any one of us do? We choose the punishment-free alternative. It's a rather natural, though not always laudable, way to behave in the short run. And maximization of short-run gains, or minimization of losses, is the way decisions tend to be made, unfortunately. A high rate of discount seems to be applied to matters of the long run, especially when the situation in question involves the commodities of nature.

The same thing is happening with the problem of the ozone layer. Unless the range of choices is modified, or the outcomes of present alternatives are changed, there is no incentive for business firms and consumers to exhibit different behavior. Appeals for shifts to higher levels of consciousness tend to have little impact when people are asked to trade off either cash or comfort.

There are examples all around us that have structures similar to both the Shell Rock and the ozone problems. The infamous LaBounty dump site in Charles City, Iowa, sitting atop the Cedar Valley aquifer and threatening the drinking water of one quarter of Iowa, is one such example. The insanity of clear-cutting the Amazonian rain forests so cattle can be raised to supply the American fast-food chains is another. The heavy expenditures on arms leading to a burdensome national debt is still another, as is the fertilizer and pesticide runoff from farm land into water supplies.

What we need is some way of bringing the future back to the present, and financial discounting through benefit-cost analysis has not yet accomplished that in the majority of cases. It starts to become clear that a democracy and its attendant market economy have a difficult time dealing with such matters.

Finally, in the case of the Shell Rock, it came down to individuals and threats. The mayors and civic leaders of towns on the Shell Rock got mad. People along the northern part of the river formed "The Friends of the Shell Rock." Otto Knauth, a *Register* writer and outdoorsman, did a series of articles on the river and the nonsense going on over its demise. The *Register* ran a hard-nosed editorial indicting just about everyone, and Representative (now Senator) Charles Grassley called a meeting and demanded action.

The outcomes of the various alternatives confronting Albert Lea were shifted, due to public pressure, threats of lawsuits, and the like. So the new sewage treatment plant cost $33 million and came on-line in 1983. It's interesting to note that the degradation of the river caused no fall in GNP, but the construction of the sewage treatment plant to clean up the water did result in a tidy upward bump to our national accounts. Apparently we can dramatically increase our revered measure of success simply by spending to erase what never was debited.

The new plant appears to be doing the job. A report

on the Shell Rock, the result of a major study involving both Iowa and Minnesota, was published in the spring of 1987.

The data show that the new treatment plant has improved the water quality of the entire river. In fact, the quality of the water flowing from the plant is much better than what is flowing out of the lake. Walleyes and northern pike have been collected just below the plant, and a few channel catfish, which are highly intolerant of poor water quality, are starting to appear in the upper reaches of the river. The water quality has improved enough that fisheries personnel are now stocking smallmouth bass in the area around Rock Falls.

But problems remain. First, Albert Lea Lake is in shabby condition. The average depth of the lake is only four to five feet, with a soft bottom composed of years of sewage deposits that provide a nutrient-rich environment for algae. When the lake floods, the algae are washed into the Shell Rock, and the river takes on a green cast down to Northwood.

The second problem has to do with agricultural pollution. There are detectable amounts of atrazine in the water. Furthermore, a continual runoff from farm land leads not only to nitrogen pollution but also to siltation and the brownish color of the river for its entire length.

It appears that most of the problems assaulting the river are reversible. Siltation may be the exception, at least within any reasonable cost range. But other problems have a doomsday quality to them—once the damage is done, it is irreversible. Pollution of the Cedar Valley aquifer by the LaBounty dump site, if it is indeed occurring, is one such concern. Disintegration of the ozone layer may well be another. Such situations, like the extinction of a species, contain within them a point of no return.

The rain of an August night falls on my tent, here

above Northwood, Iowa, and a few yards away the Otter
rolls gently south toward a wizard with lambent eyes telling some young boy:

> See two looks away
> And listen.
> That sound you hear
> Is the cry of your children
> Somewhere down the bloodlines.
> And you thought . . .
> . . . It was only the wind.

THE NEXT MORNING IS A CLASSIC. Dawn comes up
all silence and fire like the start of the world must have
been. Heavy fog on the river and across the countryside.

I am loaded and rolling by 7 a.m. on flat water. The
heron is waiting around the first bend and takes me
through pretty countryside with large groves here and
there. But mostly the riverbanks are pasture. Herds of
cattle, wary and wondering, watch me go by. The guys
mowing the grounds of the Northwood Country Club
wave as I pass below them, and I am in Northwood at
nine.

Here the river flows through Swensrud Park, a pretty
place. It's easy to see why the people of Northwood were
furious about the pollution of the Shell Rock. They obviously care about the river. The park is designed to com-
plement the long curve of water through the town.

A couple of portages are necessary past some shallows where a small bridge is being constructed and where
another bridge is built only a few inches above the water.
Bob With-A-Norwegian-Sounding-Last-Name is with a
construction crew and helps me with the first one. I ask
him about the condition of the river. He believes it is im-

proving, though he wishes the greenish color would disappear. He also says people are starting to catch some gamefish south of town.

By 11 a.m. I am standing on a sandbar just below the second portage and thinking. Before starting out on this voyage, I scouted the river by car. My notes say that the stretch I am entering should be covered in early morning or late afternoon, if the day is warm, since the river flows mostly through open pasture and fields all the way to Plymouth, which is about a six-hour paddle.

It's warm, all right, even after the storms of last night washed away much of the humidity. But, since it's early, I push on.

My notes are correct. The Shell Rock flows like a flat highway for miles between corn fields planted right up to the water's edge. I fall into a trance-like state—three strokes on the left, three on the right, three on the left, three on the right, hour after hour.

In the heat, I am comforted by the knowledge that J. Clark Salyer was here before me, on July 14, 1932. He was doing work for the Zoology Museum at the University of Michigan, and his field notes in a rough-hewn script read: "July 14, 7:00 p.m., air temperature 90, no shade, no cover, open pasture, bass rising in late evening."

In the midst of the Great Depression, in the heat of an Iowa summer evening, Salyer was here along the Shell Rock. Fascinated with juxtaposition, I turn over the image in my mind of bread lines forming in the great cities while J. Clark Salyer carried on the work of science along a small river in a smaller time. On the whole, I would rather have been with him, watching the bass rise.

I am swinging back southeast and pass under Highway 65 again. This portion of the river is the longest stretch without a town, with the exception of the Glenville-Northwood run. Kensett and Manly lie to the west, but the Shell Rock ignores them and tends to its own business.

In mid-afternoon I have a pleasant surprise. Limestone has gradually being making an occasional appearance along the shore, rising several feet above the river's surface. In shallow places I can feel rocks with my paddle instead of mud or sand. And as I come down a small, fast rapids, the current takes me within two feet of a limestone ledge on the shore and pushes me into a half-mile long reach of heavily forested, low limestone banks.

A fast-running stream, Elk Creek I think, enters from the west, and the trees arch over the river to form a cool tunnel. I walk up the creek a ways and discover a grove of mature oak trees. A half-grown duck is resting in the weeds along the creek, is startled by my appearance, and makes a pathetic attempt at flying.

No luck. She rises three feet into the air just in front of me, crashes back into the water, embarrassed I suppose, and flaps away up the creek in an inelegant run-fly-bounce flurry of water and feathers. Pretty much like I operated at that age, I remember, when the bullies came by.

Back in the canoe, I am close to the shore, in shadow, and within a few yards of a muskrat perched on a flat rock before I see him. He has seen me, though, and has gone into a crouch with his head between his paws. Sort of an "if-I-am-real-still-and-real-quiet-I'll-be-all-right (I hope, I hope)" routine. I drift by within four feet of him, continue on for another five yards, and swing the canoe around for a picture. That's too much. The little guy is off the rock and into the water.

I am taken with this place. Here, far from any town, are forest and deep water and abundant signs of wildlife. I consider camping, but pursuit of goals dominates trusting the moment all too often in my life, and it does just that here. I move back out into hot sun, regretting immediately that I did not stop and remembering Loren Eiseley's words:

> Today I skirted the storefronts in the rain
> hurrying as men always hurry
> from one future to the next . . .

Within an hour, though, the Shell Rock has completely shed its upriver character. The bottom is rock and gravel, the current much faster. There are many long riffles that take me through bend after bend, and just as I come around one of those bends in the late afternoon, I see something that causes me to pull up sharply.

Twenty yards ahead are a half-dozen cows out in shallow water. Another thirty with calves are on the bank. None of that bothers me much, since I have been traveling past cows and calves for most of the trip. What does bother me, though, is that directly in the middle of the stream, standing in about a foot of water, is a brown bull as big as my old Dodge van. An Iowa rhinoceros.

His head swings up quickly as I come into view, while I back paddle into a little cove. Staring at me, he is of no mind to move. I stare back. There we are. Two old bulls in the water, looking at each other, in the middle of Iowa, on a summer afternoon, late in the day, late in the century, late in our lives.

Looking downriver, I can see that the channel is on the left side, near the shore. Going through there will take me within ten feet of my colleague, who looks mildly disturbed and potentially hostile. The cows gather around him to watch me, and he seems to fluff himself up to even larger size as they do.

A fleeting vision has me taking off my red shirt, draping it over the paddle, sticking a coneflower in my teeth, and having it out with him, right here and now. But the sound of Spanish trumpets fades quickly, and the murmur of the expectant crowd I thought I could hear dies away. So I just wait.

After twenty minutes, he decides I am not worth the effort and moves slowly up the opposite bank followed by the cows. He declared victory, got out, and I hustle by, defeated and heading for Plymouth.

More riffles and limestone ledges. Fast water and deep pockets below the rapids. I make a mental note to think about how Iowa let the opportunities for this kind of place slip away. For now, I concentrate on getting through tricky water.

I have been hot before, but never hotter than I am right now. Nine hours of sun and bulls and fences and paddling have me searching for a spot to camp. Three-quarters of an hour below the bull, a limestone ledge protrudes into the river.

It's about twenty feet long and ten feet wide, forming a natural wharf. Up the bank is a level area for my tent, and the heron is standing around fifty yards downstream, so I figure this is it.

I strip off my clothes, grab a beer that's as warm as I am, walk out into the fast water, and lie down. The bull and the wire, the miles and the heat, drift away. In case you have ever wondered about its exact location, nirvana can be found on a limestone shelf in the Shell Rock River, just above Plymouth, Iowa.

My campsite is high on the west bank, hard by where Lt. Albert M. Lea and his United States Dragoons camped one summer evening in 1835, before crossing the river and heading east the next morning. He wrote about Iowa in his journal.

The general appearance of the country is one of great beauty. It may be represented as one grand rolling prairie, along side of which flows the mightiest river in the world, and through which numerous navigable streams pursue their devious way towards the ocean. In every part of this whole District, beautiful rivers and creeks are to be found, whose transparent waters are perpetually renewed by the springs from which they flow.

In the still, clear night a small plane hums northward under the stars. Later a big jet does the same, and there are village lights far to the east. I lie in my tent and wonder what Lt. Lea's Dragoons would think of a river no longer transparent and how his point rider would have handled the wire. I wonder what Lea would think about the dead lake bearing his name. Outside, the river works its way south with noisy enthusiasm.

OVERNIGHT, IOWA HAS CHANGED. Yesterday it was summer. While I slept, autumn came. The sound of the tent flapping awakens me at 5 a.m. to a cool, gusty wind and gray skies, with clouds sprinting from west to east.

The river has changed, too. A sluggish caterpillar in southern Minnesota has now become a butterfly. Just below Plymouth, the flat banks rise into limestone cliffs twenty or more feet high. The wire sullying the river is gone, the current is swift across a rocky bottom, and the Shell Rock flows with abandon around sharp bends and over ledges the size of small dams. The Solitude senses the change and wants to participate. I must hold it back a little or these miles of beauty will pass too quickly.

Drift from the pre-Illinoian glacier passes beneath my hull as I blow around a curve where Rock Falls Creek enters the river on my left. On the west bank is Camp of the Woods, with recreational vehicles and tents resting in shady campsites. I stop to talk with the owners, but they are out, leaving a sign on the office door that says: "Hi, we've gone to town. Just pick any spot. We'll see you later." A soft Iowa approach to things.

Just below the camp is where Winnie Watkins died thirty years ago. She was the great aunt of my friend Curt Cornell, and he speaks of her lovingly. She married a railroad engineer and lived in Omaha. But her summers were spent with Iowa relatives, fishing along the Shell Rock.

Day after day, year after year, in her bib overalls, flannel shirt, and floppy hat, she fished this stretch. They found her lying in the river she loved. She died of whatever old age sometimes does and simply tumbled forward into the water. In this place of silence, I tip my hat to Winnie Watkins.

Right above Rock Falls are remnants of the milldam Elijah Wiltfong built when he and his family settled here. A narrow passage on the right side of the dam looks passable by canoe. I back the Solitude upstream to position it for the chute, dig in hard to pick up speed, and go over the top.

As I hit the drop-off, the bow slants down at a thirty-degree angle, dips into the foam, and water comes into the boat. There is a moment, just a moment, when I wonder how far under the bow will go; but the stern clears the lip of the dam, the bow bounces up, and away I go under the town bridge with a little water sloshing around the gear.

Rock Falls feels right to me. I have seen towns like this in the White Mountains. Quiet, perched on cliffs above the river, 148 people minding their own business. Villages don't come much prettier than this one.

Across the river from what passes for a main street is Wilkinson Pioneer Park. If you're into what is called "modern camping," as opposed to "primitive camping," this is your spot. It's right on the river and has good roads and a covered bridge, to boot.

Best of all, though, it's noon and time for the Rock

Falls tavern to open. The boys with their shirts off in the large corner booth are building new grain bins outside of town, according to Lois Fingalsen who is tending things. The blackboard says today's special, at $2.45, is beef stew on a biscuit, with bread and butter (forget the redundancy; it's carbohydrates that matter when you're canoeing or building grain bins). I'll have that and a cold Bud.

A regular one, too. None of that light stuff tasting like river water. Real cold. It's been two-and-a-half days since I have drunk anything other than warm liquids, and just the thought of a cold beer can send me reeling with ecstasy. Mrs. Fingalsen seems to move in slow motion as she opens the cooler, takes out the beer, and removes the cap.

And the stew is just as good. While I eat, I talk with her about Rock Falls. Aside from a few houses, what else goes on here? Well, there's the lounge, the post office, and a store selling recreational vehicles. The locals do their shopping at the supermarkets and malls in Mason City.

A boy in the park has told me that sometimes 400 tubers come splashing down from Plymouth on a summer Sunday. Any thought of an art colony? It's a perfect place. Fine river, scenic, nice park, paved roads in and out. I've seen similar places in Vermont, not half as pretty as Rock Falls, thick with visitors just because some enterprising folks encouraged artists and antique dealers to set up shop. How about combining that with a farmers' market? "No," Lois Fingalsen replies, "nobody's ever brought that up."

The second beer is only slightly less joyful than the first, and I nap in the park on a picnic table afterwards. There is something about wire across the water and a prime river mostly empty of fish in its northern reaches and a remarkably beautiful town like Rock Falls languishing that all fits together. I think about it as I lie in Wilkinson Park with autumn coming on.

The high cliffs, a 375-million-year-old legacy of the Upper Devonian geologic period, flow on and on through the Shell Rock River Greenbelt. The cliffs were here 300 million years before the last dinosaur died.

Between 1960 and 1975, the Cerro Gordo County Conservation Board had the uncommonly good sense to acquire 590 acres of contiguous land along the Shell Rock between Rock Falls and Nora Springs. It's the way a river was meant to look—miles and miles of riffles, then quiet water, then more riffles and bends and cliffs. Shady banks and no cattle sloshing up and down, in and out. Farms visible only now and then.

Ferns and moss and flowers grow from the cliff faces, and I respect their grit for hanging on in tough places. On top of the cliffs there are large oaks, small conifers, and hickories. A green heron fishes her way through the afternoon, red-winged blackbirds complain about my coming, and a red-tailed hawk drifts in the western sky.

In places, the cliffs undulate, are scalloped so deeply from forces only the Wizard understands that you can hide a canoe in the indentations. Hanging onto the limestone in one of the scallops, I feel a presence of some kind and decide to stay the night.

I make camp on a bend, where the Shell Rock turns south after flowing east for a short distance. The sky has cleared, the sunset is magenta. I lean against my rolled-up sleeping bag in front of the tent and look down the river.

Here, somewhere above Nora Springs, Saturn is 30 degrees up in the southern sky, yellow-orange, and I am comforted by its presence. I begin to sing a little chant.

> Oh wind come again
> Wind come again
> And the wind always comes when I call . . .

Over and over I sing it, and the Wizard hears. Just across the river, though I can't quite see him in the blue dusk, he is busy putting the land to sleep, says good night to a sleeping butterfly, and waves at an evening bird.

He's an elusive fellow and never talks with me directly. His preference is for things non-linear, matters of shape and sound, of shadow and color. There are, you see, dancers and dreamers, and he is a little of both, dealing in a currency of flow and transformation and purpose so crystalline it escapes us. He operates just at the nexus where reason and magic collide.

But in his own fashion, he has given me a word. Paddling a canoe, the rhythm of your stroke, over long miles of flat water is on the order of a mantra, an incantation, a prayer repeated until layers of consciousness are pealed back like the opening of an onion to its core.

The word is "enlightenment." For some reason, it sort of sidled into my consciousness uninvited. Ideas sometimes do that. I was paddling and thinking about Iowa and left the door half open. And like a brush salesman of old hoping for some lemonade on a hot afternoon, the word rapped gently and came on in when I was too tired to resist.

Once I sat in a soft chair, in a house on the Maine coast. A man from Yale University asked where I was from. When I answered him, he became earnest, in the way some easterners do, and excitedly told me about his research. He was studying patterns of thought in the United States and had divided the country into regions. By his criteria and by ways that escape me now, he had determined that the region in which Iowa is located demonstrably produced the clearest thinking of any region. While he treated me in a way exotic specimens are handled, I told him I could not agree more.

I'm not sure I still agree, though. Somewhere along

the way we capitulated. We forgot about that marvelously clumsy word "usufruct." The word's Latin origins mean, quite literally, "use of the fruit." Fully defined it means this: the right to utilize and enjoy the profits and advantages of something belonging to another so long as the property is not damaged or altered in any way.

There was a time, I think, when most Iowans understood usufruct. Then we started getting bad advice. Some of it came from the land-grant colleges, from professors who are all too cozy with big government and big industry, in the way that professors of business often are. Things got muddy and dispassionate advice was hard to find.

That always happens when universities get dragged too far into the affairs of the world and consulting replaces thinking. Pretty soon we were listening to words and phrases like "agripower" and "agridollars" and "agribusiness," along with "food as a weapon." Former professor and Secretary of Agriculture Earl Butz took all of this in, mulled it over, and advised us to "plant fence row to fence row."

We became macho. The images and words toughened up. Assault replaced nurturing. Big farms, big equipment, big credit—Bladex, Lasso, atrazine, kill, destroy, put it in and yank it out, whatever the cost to the future.

Farming became an extractive industry, like mining, rather than the ancient and honored practice of husbandry. Production took precedence over care and maintenance. Usufruct was forgotten. It now requires two bushels of Iowa soil, via erosion, to produce one bushel of Iowa corn.

Wendell Berry's writings on this subject make the stomach churn. He points out, simply, that we are not living off the interest; we are consuming the principal. Usufruct means living off the interest. If you listen, you can hear the wailing of the generations down the bloodlines.

There are undoubtedly people who would revel at the thought of somehow using nuclear missiles in farming. It would be the ultimate way to really show nature who's boss. And the fertilizer, pesticide, and defense firms could hold joint conventions with agri-assault strategists as the main speakers.

In all of this, Iowa has become something like a colony in an imperial empire. Our resources are ravaged for the mercantilistic satisfactions of powers far away, powers that could care less about the rights of those Iowans yet to come. The debate over fetus rights is intense. I see no reason why a debate over those being disenfranchised by our current treatment of nature should be less so.

We need to recapture enlightenment and use it to produce a vision for Iowa. A vision that involves goodness, kindly treatment of the land, the survival of our rural communities, and yet somehow figure out a way to make a reasonable living at the present time. The vision must explicitly involve usufruct. More than that, it must countenance restoration. We're missing something.

That something is a vision guided by enlightenment. Enlightenment has two levels, in my way of thinking. One is the possession of knowledge and a sense of truth. The other is more spiritual, softer, and has to do with the application of knowledge in a way that combines the best of both intellect and feelings. The result of the first level is understanding. The outcome of the second is vision.

Some may love Iowa as much as I, but none loves her more. And if I were going to work on the problems besetting Iowa, I would start with the notion of enlightenment and how that enlightenment might be used to create vision. A vision for Iowa.

If that is done, everything we might want will follow

as easily as my little blue boat swings around the bends of Otter River. I can hear the snorting of so-called hard-headed politicians reading this. "Enlightenment? Nonsense." "There's nothing the matter with this state that $5 corn or a few smokestacks won't cure."

Wrong. Absolutely and finally wrong. We are adrift, floating without purpose through time. Caught between eras and growing older, we do not deal in an enlightened way with our problems for three reasons.

First, our educations have not prepared us to grapple with the complexity of the issues confronting us. In spite of our literacy rate and national rankings on various kinds of multiple-choice tests, we remain uninspired and helpless. In many ways, artists and musicians are better prepared than graduates of law schools or business schools, or, for that matter, most of the liberal arts disciplines, to handle the problems before us.

Second, there is the natural human tendency to retreat from that which seems threatening or overwhelming in its complexity. This we have done. Finally, the nature of American political reality has, and this is a bit of a generalization, lured mediocre people who play to keep from losing, not to win. And we are left without enlightenment, without vision, for there is risk in all of that. Not just the hazard of loss, but also the risk of exposing one's soul and substance to inspection by all.

But the fire has burned low, the cliffs tower above in the dark, and it's time to check the double half-hitches holding the Solitude steady in the fast current below me. Saturn is fading as the night moves on, and there are clouds in the north.

THE WIND HAS COME UP DURING THE NIGHT. Rain falls for several minutes at five-thirty, just as I awake. It's raw, about 40 degrees, and nothing seems right until the coffee water is hot. After that, everything is tolerable. In the cold, I am warmed by Kaye Don Young's fine words about camping on the Shell Rock.

> . . . and my breath cloud at 5:00 a.m.
> like Baez at Woodstock. . . .

The land still sleeps, and the Wizard rests, as I swing the bow into early morning water, heading for Nora Springs with the heron flying along before me.

More cliffs and riffles on the way. And some huge boulders here and there called "erratics" by geologists to mean they are of different composition than the rest of the rocks in a particular drainage basin. They seem to fit in pretty well, though, at least to my eyes.

There is one last and very swift rapids, with a cliff face on the left. As I come through, it is much like riding an old Flexible Flyer sled down the winter hills of Iowa. As suddenly as level ground slows even a fleet sled whose runners were waxed with bread wrappers in bright winters past, so I complete the rapids and enter the mill pond stretching upstream behind the Nora Springs dam.

The next hour demands hard paddling in almost still water, but the killdeers like the mud flats. So does the white crane stalking fish in the shallows. One hundred yards up from the dam, I turn left toward an old concrete landing on the east bank, digging in hard against the surprisingly strong drag of the water toward the dam.

The portage is across a narrow footbridge spanning what used to be a mill race, past the foundations of the old flour and lumber mill, and through a grassy park to the water.

Edward Greeley, so the story goes, courted the fair Elnora. She was restless though, like a bird in late summer, and turned him aside. Still, he gave the town her name. It was later combined with a tribute to the hundred or so sulfurous springs sprinkled through the area. By design or chance, then, the rose grew 'round the briar, or at least the sulfur, and the town was named. And I wonder if Elnora was as fair as Rantchewaime, wife of White Cloud, chieftain of the Ioways who passed here before me?

I am under the Highway 18 bridge at noon and the Chicago, Milwaukee, St. Paul & Pacific railroad trestle a few moments later. Just below is a 124-foot-long iron bridge with a timber approach. Settlers forded the Shell Rock here, until the bridge was built 100 years ago.

Bridges and trains, lots of them. Nora Springs must have been quite a place in 1900 when ten passenger trains a day chuffed through here. There is a faint whiff of old creosote and sadness near the bridges, where the fast mail flew and the free riders sang of morning sun and endless rails stretching clear to a New Jerusalem.

The portage and a restless sleep last night have tired me. So I decide to stop in early afternoon, just downriver from Nora Springs. The day has warmed, and I nap on a hillside under a tree near where my tent stands, while a woodchuck peers at me from a nearby meadow.

With late-night coffee in hand, I pull my rain slicker on over a heavy sweatshirt and build a small fire as the temperature descends into the 40s. I contemplate the tree beside me.

The maple has three large branches above the trunk. Suppose, I fancy, we could turn it upside down. On the trunk I'll fasten a sign that says "The Condition of Iowa and Its People." Next, a sign for each of the three branches below. The first will read "The Economy." A second says "Culture and the Arts." The third one? I'll label it "Protection and Enhancement of the Natural Environment."

Suppose I could take a walk along the branches up toward the trunk. What might the paths be called? Well, each of the elements on the branches influences "The Condition of Iowa and Its People," so I guess each of the paths could be called "Influences."

I walk along the "influence" paths and think, "We already know this, in a vague way." The economy, art and culture, and our natural environment all affect us as a whole. To understand that much is called education, as we commonly think of it.

I walk the other way on the tree, down toward still smaller branches. Under the "economy" sign there are other signs. One says "Business and Industry." Another reads "Agriculture." Still another is labeled "Government." And below these smaller signs are even smaller ones, and more below these. The same is true of other parts of the tree. In the firelight, little signs flash all over.

Finally I see what is missing. It's exactly what's wrong with Iowa and the thinking of the people who purport to govern it. We need a better metaphor. Thinking is always limited by the quality of our metaphors, and this is no exception. What's missing is a set of intricate connections among the three main branches of the tree below the trunk.

Okay, we need a tree for our times. It's just like the upside-down maple, except there are other branches growing horizontally between the three main branches. Now there are strong and direct connections among the economy, art and culture, and the natural environment. Each of these influences one another, and the totality is influencing "The Condition of Iowa and Its People."

To understand these connections is enlightenment. To grasp how they might, as a unified whole, be turned to forging an Iowa composed of the old and the new, an Iowa that breathes of civilization in its most profound sense, is vision.

The Solitude sleeps by the water. I will do the same in

this time just before autumn. Far in the distance is the lonely thump of a single drum from the high plateaus of Asia, and I remember the words of one John Briggs:

> Iowa is very very old,
> As old as the hills and older.
> So old, in truth, is this fair land
> That no matter at what period
> The story is begun,
> Whole eternities of time
> Stretch back to ages still more remote.

In the night, I dream of riders in long coats turning south in November. And of a young woman dancing in the dust behind them . . . a yellow feather in her hair.

THE CRICKET OF EARLY MORNING IS TACITURN. Carrying neither bag nor camera, he sits on wooden trim covering the Solitude's stern flotation chamber and watches me tie down the gear. I query him about his destination and gently raise the question of fares, indicating all the while that I will be of a negotiative mind. When he is unresponsive, I shrug and push off, heading downriver for Rockford.

A thousand paddle strokes put me at the remains of Whitesell's Flour and Saw Mill. Just below the ruins of the mill, which was built in 1858, are the remains of an old bridge. I listen hard and hear the shouts of greeting, the sound of the mill, the clop of horses across the bridge. I suppose Whitesell had dreams of a town one day. The water is deep and surges around crumbling rock foundations.

The delightful ride continues down a back-country river. Riffles and rapids and smooth deep water. The pattern repeats itself over and over. With the scenery fine, the river lovely, I am hardly aware the morning is passing.

Coming around a bend at ten o'clock, I am startled to see the silos of the Rockford elevator dead ahead. Soon I enter the mill pond of the Rockford dam, and the current slows to almost nothing as I pull through deep water.

During the entire trip I have been looking forward to seeing Whiskey Creek once more. Spring-fed, it runs into the Shell Rock a mile above Rockford. Dennis Parker and I camped along the mouth of the creek in the hazy autumns of boyhood.

On summer days a half-dozen of us would row our more-or-less communal boat up to where the creek runs into the river, cut the boat loose, and leisurely swim after it back to town. It was colored peeling-green and served as a floating platform for us to clutch when we tired.

I am disappointed, however. The creek used to flow with energy into the river. There was a long sandbar and a fast rapids where it entered out of a cool woodland. But the new dam constructed a couple of decades ago has created a pond that extends much farther upstream than I expected. Now Whiskey Creek fights its way into the river in a mélange of mud and swamp grass. Not a good place for the nostalgic lunch I had planned.

So I just keep going. In fifteen minutes the familiar riverbanks of Rockford are on my right side. An older gentleman is clanking around in a noisy aluminum row-boat, doing some fishing under the trees overhanging the water. I note this because he is the first person I have seen on or along the Shell Rock since the trip started. All of these miles, all of these hours, I have had the river to myself.

We exchange river nods, and I pull up behind Mrs. Swanson's place. My mother has arranged for me to take out there. The cricket, California Bob I have called him, gets off when I am not looking. He was just a lonely rider, a gambler searching for a game, and he'll catch a ride back north when the locals have been shorn.

I had planned to spend the night in Rockford, but the day is cool and cloudy. Just right for covering what I know will be a hard stretch into Marble Rock. Mother and I go downtown to Jo Jo's Cafe where hot beef sandwiches are being served.

Of course, you can always get "the standard lunch" in any small-town café in Iowa. With only minor variations, it goes something like this. Roast beef, mashed potatoes and gravy, green beans, two slices of bread with butter pats, and either jello or something charitably called a tossed salad served in a plastic container fashioned to resemble a wooden bowl.

The person who invented those bowls, I suspect, bequeathed a hefty estate to the heirs. Millions were sold. All of them in Iowa.

Naturally, pie is an option. I go for the hot beef sandwich, a large milk, and banana cream pie.

The memories are nearly overpowering as I load the Solitude just below the dam at Rockford. Mother watches me tie down the gear and says, "I wish I was going with you." She means it. Mother is pure country, in the best sense. The daughter of Ed Welch—fisherman, trapper, and hunter.

She was his companion along the Wapsipinicon in early twentieth-century Iowa, and they went soft upon the land. It was from her, I think, that I gained my love of the rivers and woods. Not just the palpable affection that comes from simply enjoying the pleasures of the fish and the trees and the water. No, she is responsible for the deeper feelings I have. The feelings that there is something so fundamental out here it is the root of everything.

And when things aren't going well, I think about Ed Welch. When he wasn't along the rivers, he dug tile ditches. Dug them by hand, with a shovel, in the days before there were machines for such onerous chores. He was paid by the rod. Fifteen cents for a trench two feet deep, one rod long.

There is a picture of him in the family archives. He is standing, shovel in hand, and looking down a field that seems to run clear to Indiana. There is not a mark on the field, and he must channel his way to the end of it. All the way. In the Iowa rain, under the Iowa sun, against the Iowa wind. By hand. With a shovel.

That took courage. Not to do it. Doing it was just plain hard work. The courage came in looking down that field and deciding to start. To push in and take the first shovelful required a kind of pluck greater than I can imagine. On hot and humid summer days, I look outside and think of Grandfather Ed taking that first scoop of heavy dirt at the beginning of an endless field. In my air-conditioned office, in my nice suit, in my nice career, I am no match for Ed Welch.

Mother worries about my getting through the churning current by the low-head dam. A friend of mine was killed a few years ago when he went over such a dam in his canoe. But I have come a long way, and the Solitude and I understand each other. I skirt the backwash that wants to hammer me up against the face of the dam, turn, and hit the strong southerly current like a waterbug.

I look back once, raise my paddle in a salute to Mother, and she waves. She looks small at 70, there on the shore, by the water of my childhood, where I caught the fish she helped me clean under the back-porch light on Iowa summer evenings. Forty years ago.

In thirty seconds I go by the place where I caught the eleven-pound catfish on a fly rod. That was a large moment. I couldn't get it out with the rod, so finally I just handlined it in. Running then, toward town, toward the family produce business, with the big fish's tail dragging along the dusty road. My dad, one of those strange few afflicted with a never-ending search for the great channel catfish that owned the mud flats of the Shell Rock, was proud. The breeding had been true. That much was clear.

A few moments later, I pass the place we called Flat Rock. It was here my father fished in the evenings, fending off the mosquitoes with citronella and letting the line flow from his nine-foot Calcutta bamboo catfish rod. That rod is a sacred artifact in our family. Kenny Govro, catfish purist and ace billiards player, made it. Now it hangs on the wall at my home, battered, but remembering by the slight bow in the tip the pull of a thousand big catfish in fast water, just below Flat Rock, in the days when anything was possible.

Going through Fischer's Pasture now and on to the Chicago, Rock Island, & Pacific Railroad bridge. I like Rockford. I have written about my days there with some affection. But a few years back, some of the local citizens were in need of excitement in the late winter months and hit upon an idea of questionable merit. It goes like this. We'll push an old pickup truck out on the ice and run a lottery to guess when it will fall through in the spring.

The location of this marvelous event, which surpassed even Benton County's Combine Demolition Derby for sheer, unabashed hix-in-the-stix nonsense, was just above the Main Street bridge. Sure enough, the truck went through the ice, washed down the river, over the dam, all the way to the railroad bridge. Here it remains lodged against the west approach to the bridge.

Rockford has an economic development group. If I were a member of that group, the first thing I'd do is get the damn truck out of the river. Suppose Mr. or Ms. Entrepreneur is thinking of locating a plant near Rockford. The question is asked: "What do you folks do for excitement during the winter?" "Oh, wow! Wait'll you hear this! We get a pickup truck and. . . ." That's probably more stimulation than a real high-rolling hardballer can take. Show them the library instead.

A half-mile below the railroad bridge, the Winnebago River joins the Shell Rock. This is a place of consecration. It is where the Wizard lives and has lived since all the time that ever was. It is also the place where my ashes will be scattered. Instructions for the end of things have been given to Georgia, my wife, with clarity and precision. I think about that only briefly, however, for a dozen Canadian geese are doing some sort of tribal stomp on a sandbar, and my attention turns to them.

Though I seldom tire of watching geese, it's nearly three in the afternoon, and the western sky does not look promising. As I move south, the river undergoes another transformation. What started out as a little stream in Albert Lea has turned into serious water. The river is fifty yards wide here and will be double that as I get further down.

A few miles below Rockford, Red Adams is fishing for pike along the shore. We talk a few minutes, while he watches his bobbers. They just bob, so I move on. I remember that Red is only the second person I have seen by or on the river since I started. And I reflect on all the people I know who drive to northern lakes or travel west to hike the canyons, all of them in search of solitude.

This part of the river is a place of islands, some of them a block or more in length. The limestone has faded away, and the bottom has returned to mostly mud and sand, with some runs of gravel here and there. Mature trees are on the shore, fields behind them. I pass a pair of large rocks and later am told they are called "The Two Sisters," for reasons not altogether clear to me.

Just below the sisters, I am dreaming and fail to study

an upcoming rapids with proper concentration. At the last moment, I choose the left channel, underestimate the power and speed of the current, and get smacked in the face, hard, with a low-hanging tree limb as the canoe slices through near the shore. The event reminds me of how unforgiving the river can be when you take it for granted.

Rain has been threatening to fall since early morning and finally builds up to it about two hours above Marble Rock. A stiff wind travels along with the rain, and my hope that this is only a momentary shower is a false one. While I look for a good spot to pull over, things really start to open up, and the river disappears in a sheet of pounding water.

I land on an island beach. Off go the cottons, and out of the river bag comes a rain suit. I don't mind being wet, but the temperature is dropping, and I have only one other change of clothes with me.

The rain slackens a little, so I get underway. It's hard work. The Shell Rock is broad and deep, and a strong southwest wind quarters in on me. The smart money would find a sheltered campsite and sit it out for the night. But I am looking forward to dinner at Clancey's in Marble Rock. So I pull hard on the paddle, and steadily so, fighting the wind.

Camp Winnebago, a place for boys, comes up on my left. The rain has stopped, and I grin, remembering the irreverent old song by Homer and Jethro: "Oh we are the boys from Camp Kookamonga; our mothers sent us here for to study nature's ways. We learned to make fires by rubbing sticks together, and if we catch the girls, we'll set the woods ablaze."

I was in scouts for a while as a young man, but I just never seemed to grasp the concept. All those knots and signals and things. Eventually I was cashiered out for possessing a pack of cigarettes on a camping trip and was stripped of the one or two merit badges I somehow had earned. I think the ceremony took place at dawn, in a gray rain. There was the sound of drums, I remember that, and aspersions were cast about my prospects in life. But that was a long time ago, I bear no grudges, and this seems like a good place to stop for a smoke, so I pull over.

Others camped where I stand. Some of them died here. A few weeks after leaving the river I sat on the steps of the Marble Rock Historical Society talking with Claude Barth, who has given some time to studying such matters. It turns out that, late in the nineteenth century, one Clement L. Webster took it upon himself to investigate distant happenings in and around Floyd County.

He excavated dozens of burial mounds and concluded, whether rightly or wrongly I do not know, that an ancient tribe had inhabited these parts. Whoever it was, back there in the wind and rain of some other August day, had the good sense to bury their dead in places overlooking the river. Some of the mounds remain intact. My guess is that the choice of location had something to do with flow and transformation.

The dam at Marble Rock is not to be dealt with casually, so I stay close to the eastern shore. This used to be a popular boating area, but the river was spoiled by siltation. Darkness rides swiftly on the shoulders of the rain, and I just make it in fast-fading light. The man fishing from the bridge below the dam tells me that camping is not allowed in the city park near the boat landing.

I hike uptown to Clancey's, toss my camera gear on the bar, and look around. There is a corner booth full of men speaking Spanish. Another booth is the locus of a card game. In still other booths, people are eating, and the pool table in the back suffers greatly.

Now get the picture. I still have on the floppy bottoms to my rain suit. I am wearing a wrinkled cotton shirt, and my long hair is wet and curling. No wonder that Sheila, who is running the bar, turns to me and says, "Can I help you, Ma'am?"

Well, she can. I respond, in the deepest voice a solid tenor can muster up: "I'll have a cold Bud and a talk with Clancey." She apologizes in a fluster, blushes, and gets the beer. Clancey, in the guise of Lance Muller, appears without summons from the kitchen.

It's settled with dispatch in the way things can get accomplished in small towns. Lance will call Randy, the city cop, and tell him of my need to camp in the park. Confident that all will be done that's necessary to help a gypsy from the water, I finish my beer and return to the park to make camp just inside the entrance.

With canoe cleaned, tent pitched, face shaven, and clean clothes on, I am once more up the hill to Clancey's. It's time to get down to serious drinking and good conversation. Lance materializes in red ball cap, gray t-shirt, red shorts, and white knee-length socks, crooking his forefinger to his thumb and announcing, "I've talked to everyone concerned, and you're in like Flynn."

When word gets around that I am a lonely and a lonesome traveler, the locals begin stopping by my spot at the bar to talk. Most of them are young. They are the sons of men I played basketball and baseball against in the great Marble Rock–Rockford struggles of old. I can tell by the names: Staudt, Kingery, Dolan, Lines. Their grandfathers supplied the poultry and eggs my dad bought and shipped on to big wholesalers in the eastern lands. Flows and transformations.

Clancey's is one of my favorite eating and drinking places in the world. This puts it in good company. For example, there is the lobby bar of the Montien Hotel in Bangkok. You come into the cool after wandering for hours through the heat of ancient markets, and a string trio is playing chamber music late of a Sunday afternoon.

Or Procope, in Paris, at 13 rue de l'Ancienne Comédie, where Ben Franklin, Voltaire, Robespierre, Napoleon, and others of lesser fame have dined. The last time I was there, on a snowy Sunday in January, quail on wild rice was a little over $5.

Then there's the Only Place, up an alley and next to a mortuary in Bangalore, India, where monkeys dangle from the trees overhead while a snake charmer practices his trade a few feet away, and where a turkey that will be the feature of the night strolls around the tables at lunchtime. There is something special about eating roast turkey while a cobra watches you.

Lance and Kathy Muller run a quality place and business is great. In the back, they have fashioned a respectable dining room for those of quieter tastes. But out front, in the tavern, it's a whole different world. My kind of world. The Spring Motorcycle Show, wherein the boys ride their bikes through the front door and park them, is held in the bar area.

And there was "Pete Merfeld's Famous Beer Slide," as it has come to be known. I ache at having missed it. He did it on his bare chest, running from across the street, through the front door, and sliding, like a big otter, right down the beer-lubricated floor of Clancey's.

Some say he did thirty feet. Others scoff at that and say it was much more. But all agree it was the cold-air register in the floor that did the damage.

You see, the mound builders and, later, various American Indian tribes knew something. Marble Rock is a power spot, and the place where Clancey's stands is the vortex of these forces. In a phrase, there is good karma here.

J. R. Ackley knows that. So did Robert Hullihan. Before he died, Hullihan was one of the best writers to work for the *Des Moines Register*. He chronicled Ackley's Marble Rock–based life and times in a series of late-1970s' columns. There was Ackley's 19,000-mile motorcycle ride through the warm airs of our Bicentennial Summer and his election, at 27, to Marble Rock's mayoral position in 1978.

In office, Ackley exuded creativity. For example, he dealt with the problem of a dead squirrel hanging from a utility wire on Bradford Street in typical J. R. Ackley fashion. When the residents grumbled to the mayor's office about how the dangling and decomposing squirrel was clobbering the image of their city, Ackley responded with all the ingenuity of a well-entrenched big city machine politician.

Instead of removing it, which would have struck hard at the city's funds, he simply declared a contest open, with the winner to be the one accurately predicting the date of the squirrel's final plummet from the wire. Some were not amused and indicated their displeasure in the next election.

Anyway, about 10 p.m., just after one of the boys has yelled, "Hey Sheila, gimme a straight shot of Black Velvet," and while I am working on a first-class ribeye steak, J. R. gets news of what the Shell Rock has coughed up on a rainy night and joins me at the bar.

We talk of art and music, of Marble Rock and cameras, of the river and of time. J. R. lived in Minneapolis for six years, craved the patently superior airs of Marble Rock, and returned. He got mad enough about the degradation of the Shell Rock that, as mayor, he threatened to file a class-action suit against Minnesota, Albert Lea, and, for all I know, the entire world. Ackley understands the river, cares about it, and believes what I believe—the future of Iowa does not lie in the pursuit of smokestacks.

In the darkness, somewhere after midnight, I trundle down the hill to my tent. I want to think more about Iowa, but I am tired. It was a long ride from Nora Springs in the wind and the rain. And, like the mound builders just to the north of where I lie, I sleep looking out at the river.

WITH INTENTIONS FAIR, fueled by the gentle touch of Black Velvet on a summer night, some of the boys from Clancey's promised to show up at dawn to help me with the portage. None are there, but I forgive them easily. At 6:15, however, J. R. Ackley and his mountain Afghan hound, Bacchus, come hiking down what is called "The Road To The Seven Sacred Carp." I do not know why the road is called by that name. Furthermore, I have no driving wish to find out. This is Marble Rock, after all. A special place in a land of wizards and magic.

While Bacchus leads the way, Ackley and I freight my gear up the sacred road, past the abandoned power station, across the bridge, and down the bank on the west side of the river. Ackley warns me of old bridge pilings hidden just beneath the water in mid-stream, and, following his directions, I swing well toward the east before making my southerly turn. The sun is out, the morning is amber, the wind has died.

For the first mile or so, the river is interesting. I move from sunlight to shadow and back again, down rapids and through woodland. But I will not spend much time talking about the river on my way to Greene. And for good reason. A little way down, the Shell Rock once again becomes broad and slow and deep. That's not the problem, though.

Those who had a hand in creating the green belt from

Rock Falls to Nora Springs truly were steeped in vision. Here, it is just the opposite. House trailers and weekend cottages, gathered in small developments, line the river banks. Television antennae replace trees, with the effect being unnatural and tasteless.

If people are going to build along the river, some thought at least might be given to meshing form with context. It is obvious that no such reflection has taken place, and I might as well be on a highway through the outskirts of an urban area. The Wizard does not visit this part of the river anymore.

So I shift to time-share. One part of my mind deals with the routine business of paddling flat water; the other struggles with the structure of Iowa I considered two nights ago.

There are paths of cause and effect that run from our economy, our art and culture, in which I include our educational systems, and our natural environment toward something I labeled "The Condition of Iowa and Its People." Moreover, paths of influence can be found running from "The Condition of Iowa and Its People" back to each of the three main elements just listed.

And there are similar causative trails running back and forth between these three elements. While the economy, art and culture, and the natural environment influence the overall state of things, so each is influencing the other. Cycles of cause and effect interlock the three.

In fact, it is time to do away with the notion of "The Condition of Iowa and Its People." That was just a convention to help me sketch out the subparts. The economy, art and culture, and the natural environment *are* the condition of Iowa and its people. They *are* Iowa. Then we are left simply with three main elements, each affecting the other in subtle and intricate ways, and constituting, as a whole, a place called Iowa.

A unified vision of Iowa, a product of enlightened thought and a modest amount of design, would reflect this wholeness. Unfortunately neither our culture nor our educational systems provide coherent, rigorous training in understanding, let alone managing, truly complex systems. That's one reason why things seem so out of control most of the time. Better put, that's why things are out of control.

My argument here is long, a book in itself. The major components are democracy, how decisions get made under conditions of democracy, how these decisions lead us into situations we would prefer to avoid, how our cherished market system sometimes fails to provide adequate or correct information for decision making due to the difference between private and public property, and how our current decisions are, paradoxically, reducing the range of choices we will have in the future.

For a brief sketch, however, consider the plight of our rural communities. Why are most of them dying? What do we mean by dying? One measure is population decline. Why is there a population decline? People move away, people die, the birth rate is lower due to cultural shifts and to a lack of young people in the towns. New people of child-bearing age are not moving into the communities.

Why are young people choosing not to live in small towns? One reason is the shortage of jobs. Why is there a shortage of jobs? Because there is a shortage of business. Why this deficiency? Partly because the shopping malls of our regional trade centers are filled with cars from small towns on Sunday afternoons.

Why do people choose to shop at city malls rather than at home? Because selection and prices supposedly are better. (And, according to what I hear, there is some entertainment value to be found for small-town folks in watching a few city weirdos here and there; for the life of me, though, I can't imagine why.) Why are selection and prices better? Because local merchants cannot afford to stock a broad range of sizes and shapes and colors and sell enough units to have prices based on volume-purchasing discounts from their own vendors.

Thus there is a dry rattle along the main streets of our country towns, but the regional shopping centers are filled on weekends with license plates from the rural counties. Over coffee on Monday morning, in the struggling small-town café beside the variety store that has just closed, those who spent their Sunday and their dollars in the city bemoan the decline of their main street.

This is what might be called a trap. Each of us makes an individual decision to shop in the regional trade center. There is no central power telling us to do it. This is democracy, after all. It's just that certain incentives make it attractive.

If just one person behaved this way, no problem. But with each of us behaving in what appears to be a perfectly rational manner, it turns out the sum of our individual actions is exactly the opposite of what we might wish. It's like a classic Greek tragedy. We see it happening, but it appears to be beyond our power to stop. It seems inexorable. It has a life of its own.

Garrett Hardin once wrote an article on this sort of phenomenon and called it "The Tragedy of the Commons." It's an idea worth having in your pocket.

In early New England, each farmer brought a limited number of cattle to graze on the communal ground every day. There was enough grass for all. One day, Farmer Tennyson thought, "There is a lot of extra grass. It won't hurt if I bring just one more cow." Other farmers saw the same opportunity and brought extra cows also. Eventually, through a series of private decisions, each farmer began bringing more and more cows until, of course, there was no grass for any cows.

Like a mouse that sees only the bait and not the consequences beyond, the farmers became trapped by their own behavior, even though each of them was acting quite rationally, at least in the short-term mode that characterizes most people's decision making. It's a simple idea, but a powerful one also.

The same kind of trapped behavior, little decisions that sum up to major tragedies, is all around us in Iowa. My little bit of pollution won't noticeably affect the river. My little bit of soil erosion won't affect the overall amount of good land in Iowa. My going to the regional shopping center won't affect the local merchant that much.

The fact that I plant a few extra acres of soybeans this year won't affect market price. My vote really doesn't matter anyway. I'm only renting the land, so there is no reward to me for practicing good conservation. My garbage in the ditch won't do much to hurt the appearance of the countryside. And my one metal trailer home and its inevitable antenna along the river won't damage the aesthetics of the place at all.

So the Shell Rock River gets polluted, while the wetlands disappear, while farmers inch down toward the subsoil, while the ozone layer is destroyed. You can argue about ethics and "consciousness-raising" until you're hoarse. But it's incentives, positive or negative, that really are at the controls. Alexander Hamilton clearly stated the basic idea in the *Federalist Papers* when he said: "Momentary passions and immediate interests have a more active and impervious control over human conduct than general or remote considerations of policy, utility, or justice."

And the cycles begin. As people choose to shop at the regional mall, the small-town merchants suffer. As the merchants suffer, selection and service decline even further, providing even more incentive to shop at the mall. There are fewer jobs, a lowered tax base, less children, the schools close, a sense of community is lost, and people move away or simply stay and die.

In a complex world, when all of our individual actions are toted up, Adam Smith's guiding hand sometimes becomes an iron fist. And, in example after example, that iron fist is bludgeoning Iowa.

In fact, the farm problem is itself kind of a trap. No one farmer has any incentive, outside of artificial government programs, to restrict production, as long as marginal revenues cover marginal costs. When commodity prices decline, the solution to maintaining gross income is to plant more acres and get more productivity out of existing acres. Since all farmers, acting independently of one another, plant more acres, prices drop still further.

Insidiously, the further drop in prices provides an incentive to increase production even more. Couple this with the fact that farmers must sell their output in competitive markets while purchasing their inputs from oligopolists who can set prices by managerial fiat, and you have the essence of the agricultural dilemma. The Grange understood this a hundred years ago.

What makes it really tough is that there are cycles embedded within cycles. For example, small towns always have been unreceptive to the strange and the new. In times of great flux, that is part of their strength. But it is also part of the problem now. Those who might have some fruitful ideas are to be mistrusted, just as those who use soil-conserving farming methods are scoffed at in some quarters. Creativity, by its very nature, demands being different. And being different has a high social cost in certain environments.

Still more cycles are hooked to other cycles. As

farmers till increasing amounts of marginal land, land that was never meant to be cropped, soil erosion escalates, rivers are fouled both with the eroding soil and with the immense amount of chemicals needed to bring the land into production. In addition, trees are cut down for more acres of cropland. Drainage wells are dug and wetlands disappear. This in turn decreases the natural beauty of Iowa and the possibilities for a recreational industry. Furthermore, as the land becomes exhausted from intensive use, still larger amounts of chemical fertilizers are needed to retain productivity, and our water supplies suffer even more from chemicals percolating in the ground.

It is, as I said, insidious, and it goes on and on. Farmers do poorly, enter bankruptcy, leave the land, and small towns stagger from the exodus. It seems to be nobody's fault, yet everybody is to blame. It's tragic.

This can all be turned around, if we have the will. Well, some of it can. Like the ozone layer problem, there may be certain situations that are irreversible once significant damage has been done. That's a doomsday trap, and we are well advised to recognize and avoid such traps by examining the incentives before us as we make decisions.

The Solitude reminds me that the Highway 14 bridge is overhead and that the dam at Greene is only a thousand yards beyond. I move out of automatic pilot and start thinking about something cold to drink.

Greene, unlike most towns along the river, is ready for boaters. There is a nice ramp downtown, a park on the left side by the ramp, a marina on the other bank, and another park for camping just below the dam. Large boats own this water, however, and the Solitude shudders slightly as we pass by 100-horsepower motors slung from big, square sterns.

The Green Inn, on the east shore, is featuring barbecued pork strips with mashed potatoes and gravy. Heavy on the saturated fats, but I take a chance on it. Not bad. After lunch, I nap in the park.

I am surprised. I anticipated big, slow water for the remainder of the trip. But just below Greene, the Shell Rock evolves into sandbars and islands, bends and riffles. The day has turned cloudy. What day is it? I'm losing track of things out here on the river. Saturday.

I also notice that I have been talking to myself. That started slowly about the end of the first day and has increased in frequency. Nothing very profound, mind you. Just things like, "Wow, that was a hard portage!" Or, "I wonder who owns this pretty piece of ground." Out here on my alone, the quality of conversation is, at best, tenuous.

Easy strokes push the Solitude along at about three miles per hour. There are autumn signals everywhere. The blazing stars are red-rose-pink splendid, but only green leaves remain to mark the wild ginger's earlier celebrations.

I pass a fawn. She is on a sandbar nibbling at weeds and does not run from me. She doesn't know what to make of the canoe. Finally, though, uncertainty overrides curiosity when I am within a few feet, and she breaks for cover. That event, small by modern standards, I suppose, has made the trip. I would spend another week on the river just to meet with her again.

A mile or so further on, two men are fishing from an aluminum canoe. I pass as quietly as possible so as not to disturb their lines. We exchange low-volume greetings, and I inquire about the river below. I learn there is a dam further on, though nothing in any of my reports on the river warned me of it.

I like the river here. Woods and high banks, decent current, and some of the fishiest-looking water you're likely to find.

As I round a bend, thirty minutes later, I notice the aluminum canoe is following me. I pay no attention and continue my even stroking. Three young men are fishing from a motorboat, so I ask about the distance to Clarksville. They are not sure, but guess it at about four hours.

The aluminum canoe is gaining on me; I can see it on the curves. From downriver comes the distinct sound of tumbling water caused by dams or big rapids. I bend east, see the white water, and pull for the south shore, right into the middle of Camp Comfort.

Now let me stop a minute and talk about Camp Comfort. The park is a nice one and is filled with weekend people enjoying the river. There are tents and campers and charcoal grills and open fires. Kids are mashing the water with cane poles. That's all fine. The river can't be pristine all the time, and people seem to be treating it well and having a good time in the open by the water.

But who is responsible for naming this pleasant place "Camp Comfort"? That's what I want to know. In certain ways, Iowans confirm the suspicions, most of them wrong I might add, of those who live outside the state. This is a good example. Somebody gave exactly five minutes' thought to naming this park, stumbled on what they thought was a touch of clever alliteration, and slapped on a label that sounds like some giant, outdoor bathroom or a retirement home for soldiers from the Boer War. I have tasks for the person responsible. They involve outdoor work and heavy lifting.

Fifty feet from the shore, the aluminum canoe carrying the fishermen passes me. They tell me to follow them and they'll show me where to land. I follow.

Larry and Randy of the aluminum rig are good guys. Red-faced and puffing, Randy asks, "How long have you been canoeing?" I'm not sure of what he means, so I mumble about something or other. He says they have been trying to catch me for the last hour, paddling as hard as they could in their unloaded canoe. I was simply doing my normal stroke, carrying over a hundred pounds of gear, and was unaware that any race was in progress.

But I see what they're getting at. They're talking about skill. So I point to the Solitude and say, "She flies." Also, after a week on the river, my shoulders and back have merged into a paddling machine that can run at high speed for hours without tiring. Not yet a voyageur, but getting there. I say nothing about that, however, and continue to extoll the virtues of my canoe.

It's difficult to judge whether I am looking at a natural dam or something put there by humans a long time ago. I guess the latter. In any event, there is no channel through the rocks and small boulders, so Larry and Randy offer to help me portage. Campers wave and call out to us, asking about destinations and where I started.

Larry works at a food processing plant in Ackley, comes here regularly, and thinks well of Camp Comfort. He suggests I stay the night, noting that the walleye fishing is pretty good in the evening. But, even though it's late afternoon, I have become accustomed to being alone with the river and my thoughts, so I thank him for his invitation and shove off downstream.

An hour below our camp of comfort, I can hear the far rumble of storms on this Saturday afternoon. Thunderheads are closing in from the west, as I start looking for a place to stop.

The Wizard of my river likes sandbars. So do I. There is something inherently mystical about them. For part of the year they are gone, then choose, like a great blue whale clicking along below the surface, to breach in low-water time. They are fun for swimming and fishing, but camping on them means you spend an extra half-hour the next morning removing sand particles from your gear.

And flash floods somewhat diminish their value as a campsite.

Nonetheless, toward dusk the Shell Rock presents a long curving sandbar with plenty of driftwood and I decide to spend one night of the journey there. I fasten down the tent by tying the ropes to logs and the canoe, gambling the approaching storms will pass around me.

With a small fire going and the thunder moving off to the north, I feel better. As usual, I am less than excited about my camp cooking. But I get it over with and settle back into the evening, trying to synthesize what I have been struggling with since pushing off in Albert Lea.

As I said upriver, if I were going to create a vision for Iowa, I would start with the notion of enlightenment. I would create a state that is looked upon as the way life ought to be lived in an advanced civilization.

The most essential indicator of enlightenment, obviously, is the preservation and enhancement of the very natural systems that sustain us. That's basic, fundamental. Therefore, the condition of the natural environment is a good proxy measure for the quality of spirit, intelligence, and enlightenment of a state.

Animals do not foul their own nests, yet a state that boasts about its academic prowess, as measured by standardized multiple-choice tests, has reduced its timber stock by 75 percent in 100 years (only Nebraska, Kansas, and the Dakotas are more barren than Iowa), has allowed 60 percent or more of its soil to erode, and now adds wretched water quality to that list.

Are we really surprised that people leave Iowa or refuse to come here? Does it ever strike you that academic test scores might not be measuring anything very important about the ability to deal with real problems of complexity?

For a long time, there has been a sense of estrange-

ment—if not outright hostility—between environmentalists and those who tout something called "progress" in the
form of unrestrained economic growth. Over and over
again, I have seen people who pound the drums of economic development bristle at the mention of the natural
environment. To some, the very notion of caring for the
natural systems about us seems anathema to economic
progress. They assume the ostrich-like stance that, somehow, our water and earth and trees and animals will be
provided for, if only we can get one more industry into a
city.

Or, worse yet, they see nature as something to be
dominated and exploited, a product some say of our Ju-
deo-Christian heritage. It's possible to find biblical pas-
sages that can be interpreted as supporting human
domination of nature. But such interpretations should not
be taken seriously. To consider oneself religious and yet
despoil God's world is a contradiction in terms. You have
only to sit on a long sandbar north of Clarksville, Iowa,
on a late summer evening to know that much.

Some farmers understand the notion of usufruct. My
friends Paul and Wayne Lacox do. They successfully have
practiced strip cropping on their Booneville farm for forty
years. Many do not understand, however. For economic,
political, and sentimental reasons farming has been
treated as a rather special class of business over the years.
With the increase in the size of farms and the loss of the
family farm image, along with reapportionment stemming
from shifts in population from rural to urban areas of
Iowa, this is likely going to change.

Farming will be looked upon purely as a business.
Those who continue to plunder the earth can expect the
worst in the way of class-action suits and other harsh
measures. The battle over private decisions that affect a
larger public will be enjoined. I hope we can begin to

understand the peculiar economics of agriculture and find a way to work cooperatively with our farmers before it comes to that.

If the present push for subsidy-free agriculture throughout the world is successful, more pressure than ever may be put upon the earth as farmers strive to compete without the cushion of subsidies. That prospect only adds more need for enlightenment.

As I have said earlier, economic development and protection and enhancement of the natural environment are all part of the same system. Along with our culture and arts, they are Iowa. We just have to be intelligent enough to synthesize what at the outset seem to be contradictory ideas.

A homely but profound illustration is the Vernon Springs pond just southwest of Cresco, Iowa. The pond is thirty acres in size and has been reduced by siltation to a depth of only six inches in some places. It's also eutrophic, like Albert Lea Lake. This is the biologist's way of saying it is nutrient rich, from pollutants, which means the little lake encourages excess algae and weed growth, causing it to smell and to lack oxygen.

Northeast Iowa lately has become tourist-minded. Dredged out to appropriate depths, local officials believe the lake can be stocked with game fish requiring deep, clear water to survive. So the Vernon Springs pond is now seen as having some economic benefit. It will cost $800,000 to dredge the lake.

It might be worth it, except for one important stipulation. The dredging will last only ten years if silting from the 50,000 farmland acres up the Turkey River continues. The Iowa Department of Natural Resources has not been encouraging about the cost/benefit ratio, if control of soil erosion upstream is not included in the system design.

In the case of a modest-sized pond called Vernon

Springs, in northeast Iowa, we have a small, trim model of the relationships between nature and economic development, not to mention aesthetics. It's all right there. Water pollution, erosion, economics, and the dilemma of a society that has not yet learned the important role of incentives in private decision making and how these incentives lead to consequences we should otherwise prefer not to experience.

Vernon Springs is a trap. A nasty one. Here, the misplaced incentives for agricultural production and the lack of a usufruct ethic, which I talked about far up the Shell Rock, have resulted in loss of our soil, loss of our water quality, and loss of future opportunity because of past behavior. In terms of a reasonable trade-off between costs and benefits, it may well be an irreversible situation, at least in anything resembling the near term.

And things have not changed. We are now behaving in exactly the same way as we did thirty years ago. Another Vernon Springs will be there for our children to contemplate. And they in turn will leave a similar inheritance for their children. Time will go by. The land will erode. The ponds will fill. The choices will narrow.

Unless we do something. Environmentalists, at this point, typically call for a complete shift in our values. "We must develop an environmental ethic," they cry. I sincerely wish such a change would occur. But I believe it is naive to think we will change so fundamentally. People of reasonable intelligence everywhere already have some concern about the environment. But when it comes down to day-to-day decision making, where money and mortgages and survival are at stake, it's easy to rank nature quite low in terms of importance. You see, nature is free. Sort of. In the short run.

There has been plenty of evidence over the years that our water quality has been threatened. The passage of the water quality bill by the 1987 Iowa legislature, while worthy of some praise, was nothing more than a response to a problem that was already here. The future arrived on our doorstep and provided the incentive for action. Farmers and their livestock were already getting sick from polluted water. I do not believe such a law would have been passed if a group of biologists had appeared before the legislature and merely warned of trouble ahead. After all, Rachel Carson published *Silent Spring* in 1962.

We tend to apply the most stringent criteria possible to decisions involving relatively trivial matters, such as whether or not to redesign a particular toothpaste container. In cases such as these, we tend to be risk averse, and the move is made only if the probability of success is extremely high. But in issues involving the very natural systems that sustain us, we become riverboat gamblers of the first order.

It ought to be the other way around. A truly rational approach would always employ the following decision criterion: if it appears that our action might in any way jeopardize the natural order, another way should be found. The reason we behave otherwise has to do with the structure of incentives and with the fact that nature appears to be free to all concerned. The final irony is that those who profess to be conservative in matters of finance and commerce, who propagate the idea of economic progress and things material, who study elaborate computer models of decisions involving trinkets, are often the biggest gamblers of all in the arena that really counts—the natural systems upon which our lives depend.

In spite of the problem with Vernon Springs, I believe the people trying to encourage tourism in Iowa are heading in the right direction. We have long underestimated the natural gifts we possess. In a society devoted to quantity, Iowans have seen our place as unimposing. Beauty is somewhere else. The Grand Canyon or the Rocky Mountains, maybe. To understand the beauty of Iowa, you have to scale down.

In the process of preparing for this river trip, I visited my local outfitter on several occasions. Once, while I was there, a Cedar Falls man asked me where I was going. I told him, and he responded with a disparaging "Wow." I asked him what he meant. He said I could have picked somewhere more romantic, like the Boundary Waters Canoe Area.

On another occasion, a second man queried me about my trip. His observation was, "It's too bad you didn't pick a more interesting river." He, by the way, was on his way to the boundary waters. He was frantic, pressed for time, and prepared to spend over three days driving to have four days on the water. It's a long hard road to appreciating the subtle, and these guys obviously are not underway yet. Incidentally, they are both graduates of our educational systems.

Iowa. Like good whiskey, the word lies soft upon your tongue. Her beauty is much the same. Soft and subtle.

My friend, Scott Cawelti, likes to refer to Iowa as an oasis. An interesting view, I think. In a world locked to flickering computer terminals and bent on running like hell from one future to the next, maybe that's part of Iowa's role and part of our way to the future. Maybe we should start thinking of ourselves as an oasis, as a place where people can come to find softness and subtlety, where they can experience a sense of place and find time for remembering what is real versus what is contrived.

A musician from the Bronx, Chris Davis, climbed on a bus in New York and headed for Los Angeles to pursue his music career. The bus rolled across America and passed a sign that said, "Iowa. A Place To Grow." That caught the piano player's attention. He saw green fields and good air, and said to himself, "I want to grow musically. Maybe this is the place." He got off in Des Moines, stayed, and became a well-known performer. He has gone back to New York to seek wider fame, but plans to return to Iowa. He says there's space and friendliness and more time for creating his works than can be found in the city. Perhaps we should think of ourselves as inhabiting a small place of comfort surrounded by unpleasantness.

Various images of heaven float through religions. One sect speaks of a place called "Summerland." I kind of like that. Iowa as a summerland—a place still open and free as the world moves otherwise. While others count paper clips and worry about trinkets, Iowa can focus on the gifts we already possess and can provide a place of comfort and perspective for those who have lost their way.

If I lived along a pretty river, like the Shell Rock, I would make the river the centerpiece of my community economic development effort. I would view the river as a valuable resource and treat it accordingly. I would work constantly and intensively on getting it clean and keeping it clean.

A small town can create a few bed-and-breakfast operations along the river. This is a particularly good enterprise for retired people to undertake. At the end of a long day on the river, I hate the thought of setting up a tent and cooking, except for those few occasions when I want to be alone. I would gladly pay well for a good meal, a hot shower, a soft bed, and the opportunity to meet some people in a community.

There are others like me. And there are also bicyclists, tubers, cross-country skiers, snowmobilers, hunters, hikers, and fisherpeople. Some farmers in Corning have established pheasants as an industry through habitat improvement coupled with offering bed-and-breakfast options to hunters. Last fall they booked 300 hunters. They are now expanding the idea to fisherpeople.

Michael Andorf is a farmer near Brandon who saw the possibilities there. He opened a campground, gift shop, and refreshment stand at the half-way point of the 52-mile-long bicycle trail from Cedar Rapids to Waterloo. Of such bike trails, he says, "It's a sleeping gold mine." Arvel Smith remodeled his tavern and built a campground in Graff, along the Heritage Trail from Dyersville to Dubuque and loves the business. He says his customers come from just about every state. There are other examples.

Deal with the outdoor person's conundrum: how to get back from where you started. Shuttle services for canoeists and others are needed. Put in a convenient landing for boaters and post a simple sign indicating the best portage. Welcome those who come in off the river or out of the fields or from along the roads, hungry and tired.

Be like IBM. You may not always have the most stunning product, but add service as an important attribute of the product. You may not have the fanciest or most scenic river around, but you have added the dimension of service, which makes your river intrinsically more appealing. They will come to your river or your bike trail or your fields.

A local restaurant can offer a canoeist's special on weekends. Provide some entertainment and a community tour for those you have enticed to stop for the night. Do these things, do them well, and pretty soon you'll have a fair amount of tourist dollars being spent in your town. And people will begin to say, "You know, that's a good place. I'd like to live there."

I'm beginning to think the Iowa countryside is trying to tell us something, but we're not listening. The deer population has increased in Iowa by 10 percent per year since 1980. The gray partridge has spread through Iowa to the point that statewide hunting is now allowed. We're already one of the pheasant capitals of the United States. There are wild turkeys in 90 percent of the woods in Iowa. (I know, I know. They're in some other places too.) Farmington, Iowa, supports its 122-acre city park and 44-acre lake by selling rights to turtle hunting.

Personally, I have some trouble with an economy based on killing. But I am also a realist. It turns out the one hope for conservation of big game in Africa is selling hunting permits at extraordinarily high prices to wealthy hunters from around the world. Suddenly, the game has become a valuable resource, something to be treasured and protected, rather than a nuisance to be blown into extinction. The incentives have been shifted. In a future age of true enlightenment, maybe it will be enough just to be in nature. For now, hunting is a reality and hunters probably do as much as anyone to support development of natural areas.

What would happen if a farmer decided to plug a drainage well and let the land return to wetlands? I am curious to know if the profit from selling hunting and trapping rights to the marsh might exceed what is now captured by grain farming on such marginal land. Since these wells are currently a major source of ground water pollution, it might be worth subsidizing their closure for a time until the original wetlands have returned and revenues from hunting can be generated.

I'm also thinking of parks and ponds and prairies. How many unused gravel pits or ravines do we have that lie fallow? Can water be pumped or diverted to fill these? Or do they already have springs and runoff that will keep them filled if a small dam is built? Can a park be built around this pond? Can the pond be stocked with game fish and a safe swimming area constructed?

There are other tactics, though some of them require

a little brokering. For example, the University of Northern Iowa has a fine school of music. And there are other good musicians sitting around playing at home or in bars who are not associated with the university. Why not a concert series in Marble Rock to enliven the winter nights? Schedule five or six concerts at modest prices, one a month. Clancey's can offer a special concert-night dinner. Local residents can invite out-of-town guests to their homes before the concerts or for post-concert receptions.

Other communities throughout the state have access to similar resources. The point is, if true vitality can be created in a community, it will become a place worth visiting and living in. And the point also is to make use of what we already have, the resources we constantly underestimate. As my colleague, Neil Wilson, likes to put it: "You have to sense the possibilities." To have vision is to have a sense of the possible.

Iowa seems to be of interest in the field of antiques. Can we organize an antique tour of the state or part of it? Can people on the tour camp by our ponds, in our parks and prairies? Can we provide bed-and-breakfast accommodations for them? "Come," we can say, "spend a prairie summer with us!"

How about an Iowa Trail? Something like the famed Appalachian Trail, only on a smaller order. It could follow the river bottoms from Minnesota to Missouri and visit our rural communities on the way.

Parks and ponds and prairies and trails and marshes and woods. I reel at the thought of an entire state known for its beauty and recreation on a small scale. Instead of a few 10,000-acre lakes, we can have hundreds of thousands of acres of recreational water in small, accessible parcels. It can be done, and it will work. I would like to live and do business in a place of parks and ponds and prairies, and the current low land prices make acquisition by the

GOING SOFT UPON THE LAND

state, where needed, all the more feasible.

And consider our county roads. They are fine and straight and paved; they will take you anywhere you want to go with ease. But we label them in the most uninspiring fashion. The signs drone by: T76, V14, J40. As my wife once pointed out, it sounds like a bingo game.

The Iowa Department of Transportation looks askance at giving roads any sort of names that might whet the imagination a little. In the past, we had highways with names such as the Lincoln Highway, the Red Ball Route, the Maltese Cross Trail, and the North Iowa Pike—names that made you want to follow them.

If we can't change the names of the highways, due to misguided law and recalcitrant bureaucracy, let's at least give the county roads some names that make people eager to see where they go. Run a contest in each county to get the most interesting names, with the stipulation that the names must convey either beauty, history, or both. While we're at it, can we please also change the name of Camp Comfort?

A sense of vitality, a sense of our past, a concern for the legacy of a preserved and enhanced natural environment that we will pass on to those behind us. Do this and the outside world will begin to say, "Those Iowans are smart, sensitive people. We should visit them and pay attention to them, for they know how to live and work in concert with their natural environment. Their water is clean, their soil is rebuilding, and young trees blow everywhere in the prairie wind. They are people who, seemingly in the middle of nowhere, have established a model of living for the rest of us."

If we do these things, if we become enlightened and seek vision instead of shuddering in the traces of ignorance and self-pity, everything else we want will follow almost without effort, for we will be seen as an advanced people. We will have taken small things and made them large.

And others will say, "This is a good place."

You have only to drive through the Iowa countryside on a June day to tremble at the possibilities and to experience frustration at the waste of our resources. It's all there. We simply must recapture our enlightenment to see it.

For enlightenment can lead us to understand why we sometimes do ourselves damage even when our intentions are the best. We must see that, in the practice of democracy and the operation of a market system, incentives are often structured to provide for excessive focus on the short run at the expense of the longer term. Some of this structure comes from the divergence between public and private property, where nature is treated as a free good to be wasted in the pursuit of private gain.

Thus our private decisions frequently have public consequences, such as water pollution, that in turn lead to private disaster as we try to attract industry and encourage people to live here. Our present choices, as we currently make them, consistently reduce our future options. As that occurs, as our range of choice contracts, an expedience born of crisis prevails and democracy dies. We need, it seems, a Department of Forever.

A light rain begins to fall, here on my long sandbar north of Clarksville. It is late in the night where I lie, afternoon in Bombay, and evening in Hong Kong. I think of that merely to locate myself in the larger flow of things as I drift off. And a few feet away, just across the sand, the river of otters sings in ancient tongues of other times and futures past, carrying a Winnebago song over the croak of night frogs:

> Pleasant it looked,
> this newly created world.
> Along the entire length and breadth
> of the earth, our grandmother,

extended the green reflection of
her covering
and the escaping odors
were pleasant to inhale.

DAWN IS COLORED SILVER-BLUE AND YELLOW.
Beavers are at work across the river, and Canadian geese
are flapping and stretching on another sandbar fifty yards
downriver. It takes a while, as I knew it would, to get the
sand out of my gear, and the great heron fidgets while I
work. But I am ready to go at seven o'clock. She lifts off
as I do, moving the traveler on.

A few minutes below my campsite, a remarkable
sight occurs. A long bend of the river is lined with old
cars. Not on top of the bank, on the bank. They are the
bank. One after the other, nose down, some half-sub-
merged. This goes on for several hundred yards, eerie and
ugly. They have been in place for a long time, judging by
the rust that nearly masks their identities. The newest
model I can make out is a '54 Chevy. Others are Ply-
mouths and Nashes and Dodges and Fords and Buicks and
just about anything else that ever rolled the country roads.

I have this crawling sensation that some old Kaiser is
waiting just below the surface of the water, hood open and
prepared to snap shut on any canoeist who laughs at this
ridiculous display of insensitivity. At the same time, I am
fascinated by the history these cars might relate if asked.
They went to town on Saturday night, hauled home the
groceries and the first baby, were the scene of clandestine
love affairs, and, finally, came to rest on the banks of
Otter River.

I am reminded of what Aldo Leopold wrote in his
Sand County Almanac. He said: "The landscape of any
farm is the owner's portrait of himself." I hurry on by,

thinking that Clarksville will have to spend at least three days with tow trucks, and gravel trucks after that, if it's going to participate in an Iowa of enlightenment.

Two men are talking in one of the shelter houses at Heery Woods State Park in Clarksville. They offer me a greeting, and I ask about the portage past the dam. We talk about my river voyage. One of them says it is about six hours to Shell Rock, if you're moving slowly, and adds, "It's pretty wild between here and there. You're liable to see anything down in those bottomlands. We had a pair of eagles here a while back." Just as I turn to leave, the other man remarks, "It's a damn nice river, isn't it?" I grin and reply, "It's a damn nice river."

The park is full of activity. Campers, people just taking the morning air, fishermen below the dam where good-sized walleyes are reputed to live and work. I am past the dam at nine, moving downriver in fast water by old bridge pilings and more fishermen.

A fellow in a boat calls to me, sees my long-haul gear tied down tight, and asks where I'm headed. I tell him Cedar Falls. He says, "You've got thirty miles to go by river; good luck." I thank him and start to battle a hard wind that seems to be blowing in all directions at once.

The country along here is wild, just as the man in the park said. For miles there is no sign of humans. Trees and natural meadows and high banks, and fine-looking water. Two hours below Clarksville, I begin to see an occasional home on the banks and properties in various stages of development. Some are marked, "Private Campsite."

At eleven-thirty I can see the Shell Rock water tower. More fishermen are on the river, and they are glad to see me. All ask about the trip. "Where ya' comin' from?" I tell them. The responses are uniform. "Wow! That's a long ways." Then, "Where ya' going?" One yells good naturedly, "You'll make it!" I love Iowa.

At noon, I paddle up to a concrete boat landing a few feet above what is left of a mill dam in downtown Shell Rock. The old five-story mill, one of the few wooden-frame ones still in existence, was a glory of its time. The river provided power to turn the big mill wheels fashioned from French granite, wheels that turned grain into flour with such fine tolerances that people came to the mill from great distances because of this grinding quality.

Feeling it was beyond repair and an eyesore to boot, the Shell Rock city council wanted to tear the old mill down. But there are people who care. Mike Schuldt bought the mill, is restoring it, and plans to live there, with space set aside for shops on the lower level.

The Solitude, head down and loving the fast water of the last fifteen miles, has fairly flown me here on this August Sunday. I portage around the wreckage of the old mill dam, paddle out around the shallows near the mill, turn south in strong current, and go under the town bridge.

A basic law of canoeing reads: If there is a wind, it will be in your face, no matter what direction you are traveling. But today the law is being challenged. The breeze at my back is gusting up to thirty miles per hour, and the Solitude races with it. More nice country, mostly unsettled, passes by. Mile after mile of fishy-looking river, with plenty of deep water.

A summer Sunday, temperature in the 70s, and a fine river. It's hard to think of what else one might desire. The canoe and I have become as one, an elegant machine for river travel. On we go, enjoying the pleasure of working in concert with the river's great power, as the afternoon begins to fade.

People are on and along the Shell Rock here. They are fishing from boats or the shore, sunbathing on sandbars, looking at trees and flowers.

Coming slightly southwest, I am confused by the appearance of the river for a moment. Something is strange. Ah, there it is. There is where the river ends, a death of names, of historical preference or accident.

The West Fork branch of the Cedar River is coming into the Shell Rock from the west; the two currents join and head south together. I smile, and for this special moment, I violate my rule against mixing alcohol and being on the water. Drifting along, I pull out a beer, lift it high, and toast the Shell Rock, the Otter, the River Of My Younger Days, this fine old stream that has carried me south from Albert Lea. And the river dies here on a summer day.

The Winslow Road bridge is above me. My friends Scott and Martha live just up that road. I am near home. A mile to go, 100,000 paddle strokes behind me. I know that I have traveled soft upon the land, and that pleases me.

The Solitude and I are passing through what is called the Turkey Foot area. The name comes from patterns the rivers trace on a map. The West Fork joins the Shell Rock, where the Shell Rock loses its name, and now I am going past the confluence of the West Fork and the main branch of the Cedar. One hundred yards more to the landing five miles north of Cedar Falls.

I follow a motorboat onto the slanting cement. As I do, the heron circles and turns upriver for her long flight back to the bayous of southern Minnesota. She pretends not to look at me, but I nod anyway as she passes overhead. I try to think of something to say to her and finally remember what Barry Lopez wrote about a great blue heron. "The trees said you dreamed most often of the wind. You dreamed that you lived somewhere with the wind, with the wind rippling your feathers; and that children were born of this, that they are the movement of the water in all the rivers." I think she heard me.

It's four o'clock exactly. While I am unloading the gear, Georgia pulls the old Dodge van into the access area. I am glad to see her. Tired, ready for home cooking and sleeping in my bed. Riding the wind and the current, the Solitude and I have covered twenty-six miles today.

The little blue boat goes up on the car racks, the gear is stowed in the van, and I drive toward Cedar Falls. While I drive, I remember.

I remember the wire and the bull and Lois Fingalsen's home-made stew near the cliffs of the northern river. I remember my mother on the shore by the dam in Rockford and fine times at Clancey's in Marble Rock. I remember Randy and Larry, and J. R. Ackley, and Red Adams, and Bob who helped me with the Northwood portage. I remember pelicans and a fawn and wild geese and muskrats and beaver and more trees than I know the names of and more flowers than I can count.

But most of all, I remember a cinnamon-colored river and a wizard running through tall grass on evenings washed in blue. And I am haunted by one phrase from an old Guatemalan ballad that has been turning over and over in my head as the Solitude and I traveled the long and lovely miles, chasing a vision, looking for Iowa. . . .

. . . all things are lent to us.

Thanks for coming along.

Worldly Things

Lasers, Dreams, and Real Money

DREAMS ARE FUN. James Freedman, president of the University of Iowa, has a dream called laser technology, and he's excited about it. In fact, he's excited enough that he wants Iowans to approve the issuance of $25 million in bonds to construct the Center for Laser Science and Engineering at the university.

Moreover, President Freedman is impatient. He wants it done now, pronto, yesterday if possible. Frankly, the whole thing is making me a little nervous. I have the same misgivings about any large projects in high tech, or other areas for that matter, where public money is being used as venture capital.

Notice, I didn't say I'm opposed to the laser funding. The idea strikes me as visionary, and we have experienced, to be sure, a decided lack of vision in Iowa over the last few years. But I think the people of Iowa deserve quite a lot more information on the proposal than we have been given thus far.

Twenty-five million dollars is a fair amount of money. And that's just the front end of the deal. When it's all wrapped up and the bonds are paid off, the final tally will be something more than $25 million. Quite a lot more. In fact, depending on what interest rates and amortization schedules are assumed, I'm guessing that Iowans are going to pony up $45–60 million over the next twenty years or so for the laser center, just to cover interest and repayment of principal.

The bonds will be collateralized, probably, by pledging student tuition and fees. In reality, though, the state provides what is called "tuition replacement funding" to the universities for these projects. What this means is: Keep the tuition; we, the state, will make a supplementary appropriation to the university to service the debt and repay the principal, unless the state gets into a financial crunch, in which case you'll have to figure something out for yourselves.

These are only initial capital costs, of course. In such a young and dynamic field as photonics, which is the domain of lasers, I suspect that expensive equipment becomes obsolete about every second Tuesday. Pressure will be brought to bear, naturally, to fund new equipment purchases, and the old red herring of sunk costs will be used to bulwark these requests.

The argument will run along the following lines. We have this incredible laser-technology facility into which we have plowed all this money. It is foolish, therefore, not to maintain it at a state-of-the-art level. Therefore (ignoring the fallaciousness of the sunk-cost argument), fork over the money to keep it up to date or it will be a tragic waste of a facility already in place.

And so far we've only covered the plant and equipment costs. How about operating costs? What will be the year-to-year tab for salaries, supplies, computer charges, and so forth? Plenty, I'll wager. To be fair, though, some of these costs, and perhaps a share of some equipment costs, will likely be paid for through outside grants and contracts. Some, but not all.

You see, what we're talking about here is research. We're talking about invention. And invention does not, by itself, translate into products and jobs. In the field of high technology, the leap from invention to the reality of economic growth, jobs, and expansion of the tax base can be especially difficult because of the radical nature of the inventions and the problem of venture capital, not to mention the crucial role of sophisticated entrepreneurship, which is always in short supply. Certainly, laser technology has already been applied in some areas, but we're looking at the future here, not at what has already been done.

Innovation and entrepreneurial management will be required to make this leap from invention to marketable products. Perhaps these will come along. Perhaps not. What I'm saying is that invention, regardless of its brilliance and the esteem held for it in the scientific community, does not necessarily result in jobs.

For example, consider penicillin. This was a British invention and a superb technical piece of work. What the British didn't figure out, though, was how to manufacture it. Americans did that and reaped the big payoff. Invention, I say again, does not automatically translate into employment. Entrepreneurial management creates jobs, not invention. The Japanese figured that out a long time ago.

What I think is needed, and the hard-science folks will find this unpalatable and pedestrian, is something akin to a business plan. If someone approaches a bank for a loan to start an enterprise, he or she will be required to submit a reasonably detailed proposal indicating the nature of the business, the product, the market, and estimates of costs, revenues, cash flows, and so on. Presumably, something like this has been prepared to support the laser project, but it has not reached the public at large.

Scientists reel at such mundane nonsense. "A business plan, for God's sake! We're talking about Nobel prizes and high technology and dreams and visions and being on the cutting edge and windows of opportunity and critical moments and world leadership. And this guy wants a business plan." I admit, as an academic who has brought in $500,000 in research grants and contracts over the last several years, I am uncomfortable with such practicalities.

Basically, I shout, "Trust me. I'm out here on the frontiers, and I know what I'm doing. Don't tie me down with details and justification." As a taxpayer, and as someone who is concerned about the future of Iowa, however, I am not at all uncomfortable with the notion of justification on hard-nosed economic grounds, particularly when it is economic benefit that is being touted as the reason for the project.

All I really want to know is what are the best estimates of the costs involved in getting the laser center under way and in keeping it going. I also want to know where the 10,000 to 20,000 jobs the center is supposed to create will come from. And what kinds of jobs will these be? What kinds of skills will it take to fill them? And where will they be located? And, by the way, I'm not talking about the jobs temporarily generated just by the initial construction process of the facility itself. We can generate that kind of employment by building pyramids.

I also want to know who is going to take the discoveries from the laser center and convert these into products and services that will better both Iowa and humankind. This will not occur by accident, and if left to the more-or-less random forces of the marketplace, it's likely that someone outside of Iowa will do this conversion and obtain the benefits. In other words, who's going to be the ramrod?

Most of all, though, I want to know what other things we might do with, say, $50 million instead of building a laser facility. It's easy, in a world of trillions of dollars and billions of tons and a sprinkling here and there of megadeaths, to lose track of just how much money we're talking about here.

A few years back, someone suggested that, in light of these enormous sums we now deal with, a new measurement is needed. We confront "lots 'a this" and "lots 'a that." So it was proposed that we use the "lotsa" as a new measure. Not bad. The laser project involves about fifty lotsas.

This all falls into the category of bold strokes. I sense there is a feeling in Iowa that we must be bold and venturesome now. That something big and noticeable and seemingly forward looking must be done, whatever that something might be.

But along with bold strokes comes risk. Big risk. In such publicly funded ventures, it is, indeed, the public that bears the risk. Even if the project is an abject failure, in terms of economic benefits to Iowa, those supported by the project will do well. Papers will be presented in Zurich and published in top professional journals, grants will be obtained, endowed chairs will be sat in, renown will surely follow, and perhaps even Nobel prizes will be awarded. That's all good stuff. I like it, personally. It is not, however, the raison d'être being given for the project. The justification we are being asked to accept is jobs-cum-economic growth.

Then there's the military twist, a dance we're sure to see before long. In fact, the music has already started. Freedman launched his campaign by assuring us that the project is pure of heart, an academic undertaking in which no secret military work will be done. Recently he has begun to waffle on this point.

For a guy who continually urges us all to be well versed in the liberal arts so that we may become more human, Freedman is revealing a remarkable streak of pragmatism in admitting that, yes, it might be necessary to do some defense-related work in the laser facility after all. I am not usually bothered by a little hypocrisy, but I am bothered greatly in this case.

Freedman, in a seventeen-page letter to members of an Iowa House appropriations subcommittee, recently wrote: "A blanket prohibition on accepting funds from the Department of Defense . . . would have a serious negative impact on our ability to support our research efforts and could have a serious adverse impact on efforts to revitalize the Iowa economy." Now it starts to get interesting.

At the outset, we were going to be engaged in a great and wonderful scientific undertaking. And it was believed that considerable economic benefits would accrue to Iowa from laser research. It turns out, however, that the Iowa economy might suffer greatly if we do not participate in President Reagan's idiotic Strategic Defense Initiative, sometimes called "Star Wars," which is a space-based laser defense system. Wave on, oh flag of economic growth, wave on, whatever the cost in dollars and morality and intellectual honesty.

I fear, in spite of the visionary language surrounding the proposal, that what we may be seeing here is something described well by David Brower: "Technology forges on, not from any need of the species, but from the need of certain of its more brilliant members for interesting games to play." And, interesting or not, these are serious games. If the laser operation can't make it without military research applied to the Strategic Defense Initiative, then it shouldn't be funded.

And, by the way, I don't think I'll read any more of President Freedman's lectures on the virtues of a liberal arts education. His behavior belies the rhetoric.

Earlier I said $25,000,000 (or $50,000,000 or whatever) is a fair amount of money. I was guilty of understatement. It's an awesome amount of money. It's a lotsa. So

I'd like to know something more about how it's going to be spent, what we really can expect from our investment, and what opportunities will be foregone if we decide to go ahead with lasers. I'd also like to know whether or not the Iowa economy is dependent upon the laser research center that is dependent upon secret military research that is dependent upon the need to kill. That's all I want to know. Nothing more. Just that.

[James Freedman resigned as president of the University of Iowa on 30 June 1987 to become president of Dartmouth College.]

Entrepreneurship and the
Value of the Small Increment

ENTREPRENEUR. The very word, coming from the Old French and meaning there "to undertake," has a ring of romance and daring about it. In the minds of most people it fairly thunders of risk and creation and the molding of enterprise, of change and innovation and jobs where there were none before. It will, I predict, be the next word of the hour in Iowa.

It's about time. So let's talk about entrepreneurship—what it is, who does it, where it comes from, and how we might go about encouraging it at both the state and local levels.

We have been a while getting to this point, and, to provide a trace for what I'll say later, it's worth looking at our recent history in the area of economic development, for it is a history of youth and the failures of youth, some of which we may live with for a long time.

In the process of personal development, you first try for maturity. Then you hope for wisdom. And slowly, slowly then, you begin to understand the quick kill you longed for when you were young comes only now and then, as a matter of luck, and cannot be counted upon. The way up, it seems, is more like building a fine piece of cabinetwork than plopping it all down on red and watching the big wheel turn.

So call it wisdom, or call it simply understanding the

value of the small increment—pursuing quality each day, learning from this pursuit, and trusting that the small gains will somehow amount to something. And they do. Eventually, it becomes clear that a different and more subtle algebra is at work, where things added together equal something greater than their arithmetic sum. So it is, slowly, and almost with reluctance it seems, Iowa approaches wisdom.

We started off, like the young and the gambler, looking for the quick kill, trying to lure big firms with big employment. "Chasing smokestacks" it was called, and it was pathetic. We were unprepared and amateurish. We bowed and scraped and cut taxes and offered gifts of money. Most of the time we looked like rubes in $10 suits peddling costume jewelry to rich folks. And the big firms smiled down at the supplicants and said, "We'll see, we'll see."

Then came high tech. Nobody seemed to know exactly what it was, but it looked dazzling and seductive and, well, current. Besides, it offered politicians the chance for bold strokes, and risk comes easily with other people's money. Never mind that high tech is expected to create only about one-sixth of the new jobs in the U.S. during the 1990s. Never mind that the gestation period from high-tech invention to employment is long and tenuous. And ignore the fact that high-tech jobs, aside from those in management and the laboratory, are often minimum-wage jobs involving routine assembly operations.

So the universities lined up at the trough with high-tech proposals, did some bad arithmetic on even worse data, made promises they should not have made, and generally behaved in a fashion unbefitting the supposed intellectual leaders of the state. The legislature made no serious attempts at checking the proposals against either fact or logic, and a $130 million bonding bill, with a mortgage for twenty-five years attached, flew through both houses like a fat duck. High tech sometimes resembles high cheek, it seems.

That done, we turned to gambling. Flashy, very flashy. Surprised? No reason to be. It's a natural lurch for those bereft of money or bankrupt of ideas or both. What does the list look like? Lotteries, dog racing, horse racing, table games. How about slot machines in the grocery stores and airports? Even the Mesquakies have a "tribal bingo committee."

Unless the gambling attracts a large number of non-Iowans, we'll just be churning each other's money through casino drop boxes. The result will be a new and reasonably subtle mode of state and local tribute with a little more entertainment value attached than the usual forms of taxation. (By the way, you should know that, as a serious blackjack player, a moralist I am not.) Moreover, we are going to restrict casino gambling to the rivers and lakes. Apparently, water serves in certain instances as a prophylactic for protecting innocence and virtue.

Yet here and there, the maturity and wisdom one expects from Iowans begins to surface. People are starting to ask, "What about small business?" "What about entrepreneurs?" "Maybe we ought to be a little more patient and rebuild this place a piece at a time."

My colleagues at UNI, Neil Wilson and Al Pelham and Paul Winter and Earl Brooks and David Wheelock, all of them former business executives with a mountain of experience, have been arguing in favor of this approach for years. And while, with great success, they have been quietly training and counseling hundreds of small business people and entrepreneurs, their ideas have not been heard in the larger forum of policymaking; their voices have been submerged in high-tech, big-kill bombast and a faint roar from the crap tables that live in the dreams of some.

Now comes entrepreneurship. What does an entrepreneur look like? Trying to get a handle on the salient personality characteristics of entrepreneurs is like trying to identify the attributes of great leaders or great teachers. It's like grabbing smoke. As soon as you construct what you think is a good list of such characteristics you find a hundred people who are successful in these areas and don't fit the list very well.

But let's try. John Burch, a fellow who has done a fair amount of writing on the subject, lists the following characteristics of entrepreneurs: a desire to achieve; capacity for hard work; a tendency to nurture quality in all things; the acceptance of responsibility; a desire to be rewarded handsomely for their work, not just in monetary terms, but also in recognition and respect; an optimistic bent (any time is the best of times and anything is possible); an orientation toward excellence; good at organizing with a take-charge attitude; a strong desire for profit as a way of metering achievement and performance.

Checking yourself out to see how you fit the list? People of any competence at all will have several or most of these characteristics. My own observation is that taking responsibility (I mean *really* taking it), the attitude that anything is possible, an ability at organizing complex systems, the drive for excellence (getting it done right, once and for all), and the nurturing of quality are the behaviors in shortest supply out there.

Now if Burch is even approximately correct, and his list is as plausible as the next, here's something to notice: All of the characteristics save one are what might be called "genetic/environmental." They are personal aspects of behavior that are acquired by poorly understood processes in places other than our formal educational systems or even in organizations in general.

The one characteristic that seems to be teachable, in

the usual sense, and it is a critical one, is "good at organiz-ing," though the "take-charge attitude" portion of this is up for grabs. I'll come back to this matter of organizing later on.

Notice that the idea of risk has been absent from everything I have said, even though there is a tendency to equate risk taking with entrepreneurship, and the early writers on the subject did just that. Yet some empirical studies show no difference between ordinary managers and those people we would classify as entrepreneurs.

And other writers downplay the importance of risk in entrepreneurial ventures, arguing that most of these en-terprises start very small and are bootstrapped upward a little at a time, with minimal risk being present at any particular stage. The evidence is not conclusive on the matter of risk taking and entrepreneurship.

Where are entrepreneurs found? Where opportunities exist for innovation, that's where. Entrepreneurship is not limited to business. There are entrepreneurs in all walks of life, in education, government, and health-care delivery, as well as business, though the dynamism of entrepre-neurial people is often throttled in large organizations grown conservative by age and attainment.

Peter Drucker, the respected old war-horse of management philosophy and practice, has been studying entrepreneurs for thirty years and, in his book *Innovation and Entrepreneurship*, has boiled this work down into seven sources of entrepreneurial opportunity. Some of his categories are a little hazy, and some overlap, but they are still worth looking at. I present them along with some examples of my own that relate to Iowa.

The Unexpected. Drucker considers this the rich-est source of entrepreneurial opportunity. In its own way, the unexpected agricultural crisis coupled with the change in Americans' eating habits away from red meat has provided an opportunity for a return to the broiler-hen business. Farm families desire to supplement their farm incomes, there are empty facilities on the farms, and Americans are demonstrating a preference for poultry versus pork or beef. One north Iowa community is investigating the feasibility of a major investment in a poultry-processing plant because of these unexpected developments.

Incongruities. Goat ranches, lettuce fields, catfish farms, and the like usually are not considered as having much to do with tourism. Yet *Country* magazine finds its tours to these places, normally thought of as rather dull vacation stops, booked solid. There is apparently a strong desire by people to see the more-or-less ordinary transactions of life in rural areas. In short, the magazine discovered a discrepancy between what really exists and what everybody assumes to be true. Anyone in Iowa contacted *Country*?

Here's another example. In a world seemingly devoted to concrete, circuit boards, and the roar of jet airplanes, Maurice and Herbert Frink of Waterloo saw the need for, of all things, flowers. Now their Flowerama of America, Inc., has 100 franchises in twenty-four states. Flowers. Just flowers. And a lot of money and a lot of jobs.

Need for a Change in Process. Robotics, quality circles, and the use of lasers for cataract surgery are examples here. One of the nastiest problems in Iowa is how to keep rural communities vital by maintaining their schools while affording young people the opportunities for a rich and diversified educational experience. There is a glitch in the educational process, in other words, that is having broad and severe social ramifications. Somebody's going to clean up by figuring out how to use the power of modern electronics and telecommunications to remove this discrepancy.

Changes in Industry and Market Structures plus Demographic Shifts plus Changes in Perception. I lump these three together because they so directly relate to the phenomenon of an aging Iowa. Obviously, this trend has to be moderated if the state is going to be viable in the long run. On the other hand, there are opportunities galore in the current direction. Older people have more disposable income, have different tastes, and require different services than younger folks.

People of age travel, often to exotic destinations. And when they aren't traveling, it seems they are moving somewhere else to retire. Retirement is an industry in and of itself. Ask Arkansas. Moreover, it tends to be a stable, quiet, non-polluting, and low-crime industry. Iowa is not even listed in books on desirable places to retire, even though Illinois and Wisconsin are, and that's pitiful.

It is howling testimony to the uncreative way in which the state has perceived and pursued economic development, lamenting the "brain drain" from Iowa while ignoring the economic impact of the older segments of our population. One caveat here: Some private firms have recognized this opportunity, such as Charles Colby's The Lodge of Ashworth, a retirement community in Des Moines, and innovators in home health-care delivery.

Thus, right before us we have changes in market structure and demographic shifts. Now all we need is a change in perception from the bottle being half empty to it being half full.

Knowledge-Based Innovation. This category is a little hard to deal with, since all innovations flow, in one way or another, from knowledge. Basically, Drucker is talking about that elusive thing called "high tech" and other innovations in such fields as health care and financial services. Iowa is attempting to enter the areas of laser technology and molecular biology via the pathways mentioned earlier in connection with university efforts.

Drucker has rather harsh words to say about the high-tech field as a source of entrepreneurial opportunity. While acknowledging that high tech reigns as a "superstar" in the eyes of the public, because of the publicity it gets and the venture capital it attracts, he points out: "More people have probably become rich building such prosaic businesses as shoe-polish or a watchmaking company than have become rich through high-tech business."

Furthermore, he warns of the substantial casualty rate in high-tech ventures, the long time span between the emergence of new knowledge and its applicability to technology, the extreme turbulence and consequent shake-outs in high-tech industries, and the constant need to plow more and more money back into research, technical development, and technical services to stay in the race. There is more, and our public officials in Iowa are well advised to at least read Drucker's arguments.

It's also interesting to look at the *INC.* magazine list of the 100 fastest-growing companies in America, a list that is updated and published each year. In 1986, only about 30 of the companies listed were directly in the high-tech field.

And, since *INC.*'s list is limited to publicly owned companies, there is, as Drucker points out, a natural bias toward high tech, which because it is fashionable, ". . .

has easy access to underwriters, to stock market money, and to being traded on one of the stock exchanges or over the counter." Even with these advantages in making the list, the high-tech firms accounted for only about 30 percent of *INC.*'s tabulation.

Let's put all of this together. In the 1978–1986 period, Iowa ranked 49th among the fifty states in job growth, according to a study by the Federal Reserve Bank of Chicago. Among the causes listed for this miserable performance was the lack of small business growth. And entrepreneurship is certainly an important part of small business growth. (Not all small businesses are entrepreneurial. The key differentiating factor is innovation.)

Presumably, then, Iowa wants to encourage entrepreneurship. If we do, there are four elements to the problem. First, people with entrepreneurial capabilities must be recognized and assisted. One way or the other, these people tend to identify themselves.

If the list of entrepreneurial characteristics I presented earlier is at all accurate, and it seems to echo the content of most such lists, then the major area where help can be given is in the organizational sphere, since the other characteristics apparently are either inherited or the product of one's general environment. Therefore, a second aspect of the problem is helping entrepreneurs acquire organizational skills, including how to search for and acquire capital.

This skill is as important as any of the other abilities listed. In fact, it is often the Achilles' heel of entrepreneurs. I personally have been acquainted with two small Iowa firms, both of which had considerable promise and employed a total of approximately 100 people, that have fallen on hard times. In each case, the businesses were so successful that, paradoxically, they grew beyond the organizational skills of the original entrepreneurs and suffered greatly for it.

Entrepreneurs tend to be production oriented. That is, they are good at the core-technology, and maybe the marketing, aspects of the business. Many of them, however, lack the necessary management skills to handle the business once it has grown past the point where the entrepreneur can supervise everything that's going on. And, to be quite blunt about it, a fair number of entrepreneurs find the tasks of purely managing an operation to be distasteful. They grew up in the shop, so to speak.

A third element in encouraging entrepreneurship is the provision of venture capital, and sources for this capital must be established in both the private and public sectors. Some of this has already been accomplished, with the creation of the Iowa Fund, the Iowa Business Development Corporation, and the Invest America Venture Group, Inc. in Cedar Rapids, though I have no idea of the activity level of these funds in supporting Iowa entrepreneurship.

Finally, there are the sources for entrepreneurial innovation I talked about earlier. Many of these opportunities are in relatively mundane places we surely will neglect if overcommitment is made to alluring, let's-bet-it-all areas such as high tech.

Entrepreneurs have a way of finding opportunities themselves. Yet there are an abundance of opportunities out there at any time that will go unnoticed if left to the forces of chance discovery.

Several years ago, I proposed the establishment of a think tank for Iowa—a small, politically independent, state-funded research unit staffed with hard-headed people possessing practical and theoretical knowledge, whose task would be to exercise what one of my old professors used to call "opportunistic surveillance." The job of this group would be to constantly scan the world for opportunities of potential interest to Iowa, evaluate these opportunities, and forward its findings to the public at large, including state officials. I still think this idea generator might be a good idea.

The entrepreneurial opportunities available to Iowa are staggering in number. Most of them require no heavy expenditures at the outset and will become self-sustaining as they grow. As we mature, as we acquire wisdom, we will begin to understand the value of the small increment and the power of innovation. We will come to appreciate that things of worth are built day by day and do not require the largesse of panicked state officials, whose current munificence will become the future burden of ourselves and our children.

The Importance of Vision

Keynote speech for the Iowa Economic Development Conference, Waterloo, Iowa. April 1987

I HAVE THE FEELING WE ARE OUT OF CONTROL. Iowa, that is. Like a poor swimmer in a fast river, we flail this way and that, panicked, randomly trying anything and hoping for the best.

Yet, all the while, forces that appear to be beyond our grasp are sweeping us toward a future that is something less than I think we might prefer. Though we are here to talk about solutions, and though you're probably tired of hearing about the state's difficulties, let's tick off a few of the problems, just to get under way and to provide a foundation for what I'm going to say later.

Last year we led the nation in percentage decline of population. It seems that 30,000 of us crossed the borders in 1986, outward bound, neither waving nor looking back. In other words, about one out of every 100 Iowans exited the state in a single year.

In the 1978–1986 period, Iowa ranked 49th among the fifty states in job growth. The Federal Reserve Bank of Chicago, which carried out the study providing this data, attributed our miserable performance to four factors: lack of economic diversity (i.e., Iowa's heavy dependence on agriculture); lack of research-and-development expenditures compared with those made by surrounding states; a below-average share of scientists, engineers and technicians (professionals needed, according to the study, for the emerging high-technology industries); and Iowa's small-business growth, about one-seventh the national average.

With the decline of our tax base, we are having serious problems with road maintenance. Already, 2,500 miles of Iowa roads have been declared "minimum-maintenance" roads in an effort to save money. This circumstance probably will develop into a bitter struggle between cities and rural areas for road-maintenance funds.

Iowa school enrollment has been declining for seventeen straight years. This results in acrimonious battles within urban communities as selected schools are closed. It's even more serious for rural communities as they confront the demise of their only school, which serves as the activity and cultural center for many small towns.

Our water supply is in poor shape and appears to be getting worse. The Iowa legislature has passed forward-looking measures to deal with the problem, but it is premature to judge the results of these efforts.

Soil erosion, a sacking of the very resource that has most sustained us for over a century, continues unabated. Another fifty years of this and people will wonder whatever happened to Iowa. A serious offshoot of erosion is the siltation clogging our rivers and other water resources like so much peanut butter.

Due to various pressures and incentives, our timber stock has been reduced from about 22 percent of the acres in our state to about 4 percent. Only Kansas, Nebraska, and the Dakotas are more barren than Iowa. If this doesn't bother you, then you don't know much about soil erosion or the recreation industry or the carbon dioxide–oxygen cycle that is fundamental to the sustaining of human life, not to mention aesthetics.

I can extend the list, but you get the point. What's going on is a mixture of incompetence, forces beyond our control, impatience, and a dire shortfall of creativity. Most of all, what we are experiencing is a lack of vision.

A good way to approach this notion of vision is to think about gaps. A problem exists when there is a gap between what is and what should be. To solve the problem, we must, first of all, be aware of the gap. We must also have motivation to decrease the gap. In addition, it's helpful to have some idea of the size of the gap. And, we have to marshall the abilities and resources to close the gap. So, a problem—any problem—can be thought of as simply a gap between where we are now and where we might like to be.

We can all agree there is a gap. Call it "the Iowa Gap." Furthermore, we're aware of the gap in a vague way, and we seem to have the motivation, the resources, and maybe the abilities to decrease the gap.

Yet there is a problem within a problem here, and it goes like this: We haven't defined the Iowa Gap. We have some sense of where we are at the present, and, obviously, we don't like it. The hitch is that we don't know anything about the size of the gap and how to close it, because we have not given any thought to the "what should be" dimension of the problem.

Without knowing what you want to be, it's pretty hard to move toward anything at all. Still, we try. One week it's more money for education. Then it's promising, but ill-considered, high-technology initiatives. Next week it will be riverboat gambling or, God help us, fireworks.

There's a tendency to say, "Gee, I must not be very smart, because I surely cannot see how all of this activity fits together and relates to the dilemmas before us." Don't worry. It doesn't fit together. The reason it doesn't make any sense is that we have spent no time in reflecting about what we might like Iowa to be. Incidentally, most communities operate in the same fashion.

You see, without a vision, without some idea of where we want to go, there is no way of judging the worth of various alternatives proposed for economic development. So vision is just another way of talking about the "what should be" dimension.

Vision provides us with the general outlines of how we might like to appear down the road. It gives us the means to fashion more or less concrete objectives.

The objectives then furnish us with a set of criteria, a yardstick in other words, for judging the relative merits of various alternatives that are proposed. With objectives flowing from vision, and criteria, in turn, flowing from objectives, alternatives for economic development can be evaluated in terms of how we will look in years to come if various alternatives are selected.

With criteria in mind, some alternatives will be accepted, some rejected. Those that are accepted will have the unifying theme of having met the criteria generated by the vision. Then the alternatives can be grouped into various "strategy packages," and these packages can be evaluated for funding or other kinds of support.

Now, I have spent enough time as a manager, a consultant, and a scholar studying real-world affairs to know that things aren't quite this neat in the dust of the arena. The vision and the process of fulfilling that vision will always be imperfect; there are the frustrating matters of dissenting factions and political forces, the difficulty of judging long-range risks, and the outcomes of specific alternatives.

In addition, I am wary of precise long-range planning in most areas, particularly in turbulent times such as these. Instead, one moves forward with what someone once called "enlightened incrementalism." Note the word "enlightened." Vision makes for enlightened progress, even when short-run changes in direction must be made, because always before us is the portrait of where we want to be in the years to come.

Yet with all its imperfections due to politics, change, and uncertainty, a vision-based way of thinking works and works well. Without criteria and creative alternatives flowing from informed search guided by a vision, there is no way, save costly and time-consuming trial and error, to begin closing the gap.

A vision, a sense of what we want to become ("what should be," in other words), can form the basis for a community or state development plan that describes in some detail the objectives, the activities needed to obtain these objectives, and the resources needed to carry out the activities.

That's why Iowa, as a state, appears so confused, so out of control. No one has yet articulated a unified vision for Iowa. Hence, the various solutions proposed to overcome the problems we confront look as if they are the product of a crapshoot rather than serious thinking about what kind of place we want Iowa to be. The same is true for most communities striving for economic development.

Communities are all searching for ideas. That may seem like a tough problem to many. But it is not. That is, it's not difficult if you have some sense of where you want to go, if you have some objectives developed out of a vision for your community.

Ideas are cheap. They are all over the place.

Then why do we struggle so in developing our communities, or our organizations, or ourselves for that matter? Why do we have meeting after meeting where nothing seems to get done, where no progress is made, and the level of frustration mounts?

The reason is this: Merely generating ideas is not enough. Ideas, like people and factories and farms, must be managed. Even though we call upon technology to carry us through time and space, to mount national-defense efforts, and as the foundation of economic growth in some cases, most people are unaware of either the need for managing ideas or the techniques available for idea management.

For example, in the typical complex problem, such as community development, you'll find your mind doing something like this. "Let's see, maybe X would be a good thing to do, but it sure is going to cost a lot, and Y is cheaper to do, but it's hard to tell how it might work out over time; and besides, the boys on Main Street will probably support Z even though most of the community wants Y; but the Sierra Club will take us to court if we try to implement X; and we might be able to do any two of these, but not all three; and the damn water mains are sixty years old and need an overhaul; and we'll lose all of our sense of vitality if the state demands we consolidate our school with the town next door; and Jim's machine shop could really grow if we could find some venture capital, but the bank is overextended right now with agricultural credit; and the Department of Transportation wants to cut down all of the big maple trees on Main Street if we're going to get the street widened and a lot of citizens don't want that; and I sure don't want another development group meeting like we had last week; and, 'Oh, the hell with it. I think I'll go out to the golf course and see what's going on.' "

What's happening here is that ideas are managing you, rather than the reverse.

You're trying to pound a spike with a wet sponge, when what you need is a sledge hammer. Just as we use tractors to cultivate fields and computers to process large amount of data, so we need methods such as Interpretive Structural Modeling, the Nominal Group Technique, and elementary decision analysis to make things easier for ourselves.

You probably have discovered already that just getting a group of people together in a room and shouting, "We've got to do something!" only leads to a second meeting, and another one after that, and, finally, to frustration and a reluctance to attend meetings. What you need is something like a rack-and-pinion device—something that converts rotary motion into forward linear movement.

You see, in problem-solving situations, people have a tendency to start at the wrong end of the problem. They make a list of what things they already have and try to create something out of that list.

Don't get me wrong, a community inventory is a crucial part of economic-development planning. The UNI School of Business sent forth a proposal to the state three years ago for developing an "Iowa Inventory," which was to be a sophisticated computer data base that would tell people anything they might ever want to know about Iowa. The proposal got lost at about the level of the Iowa Board of Regents and is currently starving to death, I presume, in a gray metal filing cabinet somewhere.

The right place to start any problem-solving process is on the output side, not the input side. Ask: What is it we are trying to produce? What is the output we want? Put another way, what is the vision?

Then you can ask: "What kind of processes will it take to produce this output?" Then, "Do we have the necessary inputs or resources to operate the processes to produce the output?" This is where your inventory of community strengths and weaknesses is brought to bear.

So, once again it is vision, the "what should be," that forms the basis for getting under way. Everything else flows from the answers to that question.

The vision you construct for your community should be broad and rich. There is always the tendency, a natural one I might add, to focus on the tangible, on the things that are most easily measurable, such as number of jobs or the square footage available in empty buildings or the generating capacity of the local power plant or the pumping capacity of your water system or the amount of the new capital needed for a specific project.

But, a unified vision answers the question "How do we want our community to look in ten or twenty or fifty years?" In turn, this leads to questions such as: What kind of new business do we want to attract? What old business do we want to encourage to expand? What kinds of jobs do we want in our community? What will people do in their leisure time? What role should our schools play in our lives?

A good way to make sure your vision and the concrete objectives flowing from this vision are broad enough is to think of three areas to pursue within your community. First, there is the matter of economic development. Second, consider the artistic and cultural areas, including education and personal development of the individual and the family.

The whole point of economic development, it seems to me, is to provide the wherewithal to pursue some of the higher goals of life. There is too much evidence around, in the form of marital strife, drug usage, teenage suicide, and other manifestations of personal and societal anxiety, to say that economic development, by itself, is quite enough. Make sure your community has a reason to live beyond that of pure material acquisition, even though that may sound naive and utopian in troubled times such as these.

Third, and perhaps most important, is the enhancement and preservation of the natural environment. If asked, I can talk for hours on this subject as it relates to community development. There is always the temptation to say, "Well, the environment is important, and we'll take care of that as soon as we get this community on its feet."

That misses a crucial point. The natural environment

is a key aspect of economic development. Without potable water, breathable air, fishable rivers, huntable marshlands, tillable soil, and tall trees bending in the prairie wind, you don't have much of a community. It's not the kind of place people will want to stay in or come to.

The economy, art and culture, and the natural environment are not separate entitles to be dealt with individually. They are part of the same mosaic. The idea of a community cannot be neatly parceled into its constituent parts. Each of the three affects the other, and all of them together will determine both how well a community develops and whether that community is worth living in once it has developed more fully. You have only to look at the experience of the coal towns of Wyoming or the oil towns of Louisiana to understand this.

Whether we are talking about the state of Iowa or a community or region within the state, we must recognize that this is our place, my friends. What color do we want the walls and where shall we put the garden?

Only the development of a full and rich vision provides us with the means to think about and plan for the kind of community in which we want ourselves and our children to live. It is the vehicle by which we sort and decide and guide ourselves intelligently, as opposed to letting random forces or charlatans with easy nostrums for our troubles push us this way and that.

If we try to operate without a vision, if we focus only on means and do not think carefully and creatively about what we might like to be, the means themselves will fashion a world of their own. It is likely this state of affairs will be an unhealthy stew that looks and tastes exactly like what it is—a place created by chance rather than by design. Given the option, I'll choose design over chance in development, just as I prefer to use a plan in building a home rather than roll the dice to see where the rooms might be placed.

Ultimately, vision is our guide for action and our way of determining the worth of what we will become. And when all is said and done, what we really are talking about is something more than just jobs and tax bases and the pursuit of material gain. We are talking about the pathways to a more fulfilling existence in an advanced civilization, where economics, beauty, and nature are in balance.

I will leave you with one final guide for action. It's Waller's First Law of Making Things Better, and it goes like this: If you can't count it, it's probably important.

Any vision that is worth having, that is faithful to the higher ideals of human endeavor, will fairly resound with the importance of those things likely to be neglected if our view of development is limited, confined only to that which is easily measurable in the coin of the realm or the run of the tape.

So fashion a vision for your place, make it broad and deep, and rich and true, not only to the limited aims of material existence, but also to the things that really matter in the long run.

We need to leave this place in better shape than we found it, so that the children of our children's children will look back and say, "Our great-grandparents truly were visionaries, and we are grateful that they were."